DEPLOYED

DEPLOYED

How Reservists Bear
the Burden of Iraq

Michael Musheno and Susan M. Ross

THE UNIVERSITY OF MICHIGAN PRESS ❖ ANN ARBOR

2011   2010   2009   2008   4   3   2   1

A CIP catalog record for this book is available from the British Library.

Library of Congress Cataloging-in-Publication Data

Musheno, Michael C.
    Deployed : how reservists bear the burden of Iraq / Michael
Musheno and Susan M. Ross.
        p.   cm.
    Includes bibliographical references and index.
    ISBN-13: 978-0-472-07029-9 (cloth : alk. paper)
    ISBN-10: 0-472-07029-0 (cloth : alk. paper)
    ISBN-13: 978-0-472-05029-1 (pbk. : alk. paper)
    ISBN-10: 0-472-05029-x (pbk. : alk. paper)
    1. Iraq War, 2003–   2. United States. Army Reserve.   3. United
States. Army—History—21st century.   I. Ross, Susan M., 1968–   II. Title.

DS79.76.M88   2008
956.7044'3—dc22   2007036082

A Caravan book. For more information, visit
www.caravanbooks.org.

I don't know what you're going to write in your report or anything, it's just to let you know that—and even I'm pretty sure not just for the reservists but even for the National Guard—being a citizen and an active-duty member, it's one of the hardest jobs, bar none. I mean people may say, "I have a hard job. I work on brain surgery, blah, blah, blah." Well, that's fine and dandy. But when you've got to be a citizen one moment and then twelve hours later you've gotta jump in a uniform and be called up overseas or to an emergency, leaving your family behind, that takes a toll on you. I've been in [the Reserve] for sixteen years. Like I said, the first twelve, I never thought I'd see any action. Boom—I saw two back-to-back deployments. . . . So I just think being a citizen-soldier is just one of the hardest or the hardest job in the United States, I believe.

—Ian Farber, Noncommissioned Officer, U.S. Army Reserve

Contents

Preface

We came to know the members of the 893rd Military Police Reserve Company and to collaborate on this project through circumstance. In 2002–3, we were colleagues at Lycoming College, Michael as a visiting professor at his undergraduate alma mater and Susan as a permanent professor teaching across the curriculum. Within the intimacy of this small liberal arts college, Susan had student reservists called from the classroom who by the time Michael arrived were serving on the ground in Iraq and Afghanistan. Some of these students began corresponding with Susan, and the two of us began talking about their stories of anxiety, adventure, and fear. Both of us were haunted by what we thought we knew about soldiering in Vietnam and by a concern about how the students would handle the profound changes caused by shifting from cloistered undergraduates to wartime soldiers. We began to read accounts about soldiering, popular and academic, contemporary and historical. To our surprise, we found little that drew on the voices of soldiers, particularly citizen-soldiers called to war. With little to share with the student soldiers that seemed helpful to them or us, we decided to draw on our existing expertise, Susan in family studies and Michael in public policy, to think through what we were hearing and to expand our dialogue with the student soldiers. After some time, we concluded that the best contribution we could make would be to use our positions to enable reservists, like those called from the classroom, to tell their stories about becoming citizen-soldiers, being deployed, and coming home. The 893rd is not the real name of this MP company, and for privacy reasons, pseudonyms are used throughout the project for the individual soldiers, the company, and the military posts in which they served. We have chosen to represent these citizen-soldiers in the present tense in an effort to give their voices an active form of communication. What follows is the culmination of four years of our work in a collaborative partnership along this path.

In addition to drawing on each other to make this project a book amid lectures, exams, administrative duties, family crises, travel commitments, and bouts of self-doubt, we are grateful to Len Bass, Michael Donnelly, Morten Ender, Darryl Kehrer, Robert Larson, Gary Lowenthal, Steven Maynard-Moody, Dennis Palumbo, Ken Wells, and two anonymous reviewers, all of whom looked at drafts of the manuscript at crucial moments and offered valuable feedback. Owen Herring and Robert Larson provided their veterans' perspective on the development of our interview guide. We have been particularly fortunate to have Jim Reische as our editor: he inspired us to advance the project with dispatch and provided concrete advice every step of the way. Sarah Remington, also of the University of Michigan Press, kept us on track to completion. Michael gives special thanks to Terrell Tannen, a lifelong friend and gifted writer who always knows how to turn a phrase; General John A. Wickham, who generously shared his firsthand knowledge regarding the highest-level decisions made about army mobilization during and after the Vietnam War; Bridget McCracken of San Francisco State, who often covered for Michael when he should have been at the office directing a program; and Dean Joel Kassiola of San Francisco State, whose Summer Research Stipend Program provided Michael with the resources to research and write. For administrative support, Susan thanks Lorri Amrom, whose life with a citizen-soldier has been an inspiration. Both Tiffany Zappulla and Lee Zelewicz were terrific in fulfilling research assistant requests, and Susan thanks them for their conscientious work. Both of us are grateful to Amber Day, Margaret Droody, and Jean Fowler for their assistance with the tedious task of transcribing the interviews. Our collaboration depended on meeting in person at crucial times throughout the project to develop ideas, expand on drafts, hammer out differences, and even share a couple of laughs and moments of insight over a few scrumptious though inexpensive dinner meetings in the Valencia Corridor of San Francisco. For financial support at all phases of this project, we are appreciative of the Lycoming College Professional Development Grant Program. Susan offers additional thanks to Lycoming College for the Faculty Sabbatical Program, which enabled several uninterrupted months of solid research progress. Our love and thanks go to both of our families, Birgit, Micah, and Rob, for allowing us to say far too many times that we needed to work on the project and giving us the space to do so. For the past three years, the citizen-soldiers of the 893rd, whose stories are represented within these pages, have continually occupied our thoughts and concerns, and they have changed us in ways that can never be forgotten. In maintaining their privacy, we cannot thank the members of the 893rd by name, but our gratitude runs deep, and we dedicate this work to them. We hope we run true to their thoughts.

Introduction

"Haven't Had a Break"

I just consider myself a soldier, because I try to—everybody is like, "You're in the reserves?" Like yes and no. It's like I haven't had a break as a reservist since the day I joined. I mean, I went to basic training. Graduated. Home for three months. 9/11. Deployed for a year. Came home for three months. Deployed again for about a year. So I don't know what it's like to be a reservist yet.

—Enlisted Army Reservist Michelle Colton

With the confidence and crispness developed by a seasoned veteran, the master sergeant calls out, "Companeee, 'ten-huut!" It's a rainy morning in the spring of 2004, and at 07:45, the citizen-soldiers of the 893rd Army Reserve Military Police (MP) Company stand at attention, ready to receive their orders for the weekend's drills. They are gathered in their all-purpose formation hall that occasionally doubles as the motor pool. Pushed to either side of this large room are rows of long tables with attached little blue seats that give the distinct feel of a middle school cafeteria. The company's commanding officer (CO) takes two steps closer to the rows of soldiers. Recently promoted from platoon leader to CO, he speaks tentatively as he tries to find his leadership style in the footsteps of the beloved former CO, who was moved up and out of the 893rd a month earlier. All eyes are on him when he says they have a lot of work to do during the coming drill weekends, cleaning and storing the equipment brought back from Iraq, including weapons, vehicles, and tents. He goes on to tell them they will need to pass their physical training tests scheduled for the next month. Everyone knows this means many sit-ups and push-ups as well as a two-mile run, and the CO reminds them to dress in their athletic gear rather than their standard battle dress uniforms—BDUs, as he puts it. While the activities scheduled for this weekend are relatively mundane, the CO assures them that preparations are under way for more rigorous field training in the coming months and that their marksmanship qualification tests are scheduled for the early fall. At a sister U.S. Army Reserve Center about sixty miles down the road, a third platoon, known to all 893rd members as the detachment, is receiving a similar briefing from a junior officer the same morning.

With the homecoming ceremonies and celebratory parties over, it is time for the military veterans of the 893rd Reserve MP Company to resume their part-time service to the U.S. Army—attending to equipment, engaging in physical fitness exercises, training for military police work, being tested for drug use—all over the standard one weekend a month and two weeks a year. Looking out at the lines of formation, it is difficult to distinguish one soldier from another as individual features blur together through the purposeful codes of military uniformity. Who within these ranks is fresh out of basic training, and who has just completed the company's two years of back-to-back deployments, including nearly a yearlong tour in Iraq, following September 11, 2001?

By 08:00, the announcements are drawing to a close. Just before they break formation, the members of the 893rd are introduced to the idea that the company's chain of command has authorized us, Michael and Susan, to engage them in voluntary conversations about citizen-soldiering. As soon as the reservists are dismissed from formation, three men immediately volunteer and schedule interview times, becoming the first of forty-six members to tell us about their experiences of having been called to arms and deployed together as a unit after 9/11, first in the

States and then to Iraq. Over the next five months, we continued to attend their one-weekend-per-month drills and to collect life stories of members of the company at both their main reserve center and their secondary detachment location. These men and women generously volunteered their time to reveal their experiences in the hopes that they might help the American people learn what it is like to be a citizen-soldier in the twenty-first century.

True to our promise to them, this book is not a chronicle of war but a portrait of how a group of civilians living in the early twenty-first century came to the point of being called to such extraordinary service to their country and how they adapted to long deployments while coping with family relations, military duties, and civilian careers. Like enlistee Michelle Colton, many feel like they have not had much of a break since 9/11. What meaning do they bring to being hailed by public officials and the media as America's new citizen-soldiers? How do they deal with the seismic changes in their lives amid the complexities of American life? What do they reveal about their relationships, inside and outside their military unit, as well as their thoughts about their commitments to the U.S. Army?

From "Weekend Warrior" to Full-Time Soldier

In the fall of 2001, just a little over a month following the 9/11 attacks, President George W. Bush gave a simplistic directive to most Americans, stating, "Now, the American people have got to go about their business. We cannot let the terrorists achieve the objective of frightening our nation to the point where we don't conduct business or people don't shop."[1] At the same time that most Americans were assigned the task of resuming their role as dedicated consumers, a very different set of events was unfolding for the members of the 893rd Army Reserve MP Company and the more than 186,000 reserve soldiers who would come to serve in the wars of Afghanistan and Iraq after 9/11.[2]

At its most basic level, the U.S. Army is divided into three separate components—the active-duty all-volunteer professional soldiers; the National Guard, with its combat training emphasis; and the Reserve, with units designated primarily for combat support ranging from running prisoner of war camps to providing medical services.[3] Although Reserve forces have been crucial to wartime deployments through both world wars and the Korean War, most Americans—including the majority of the reservists in the 893rd MP Company—imagine the post-Vietnam U.S. Army as the active duty all-volunteer professional force. Americans have come to expect professional soldiers to be the boots on the ground for fighting foreign wars, an expectation that was reinforced by deployment decisions made by the U.S. Army as recently as the 1991 Persian Gulf War.

Held back from the Vietnam War, reservists were popularly dubbed "weekend warriors" and prior to 9/11 were recognized as the part-time soldiers who help restore order and carry out essential services during natural and human-made disasters on American soil. In the immediate aftermath of 9/11, members of the 893rd were not surprised to have been pulled from their civilian routines to provide a sense of security and calm the public. Within hours, reservists across the nation were called up—drawn from college classrooms, convenience stores, police departments, factories, transit authorities, and office buildings—and quickly appeared in airports, in the commercial districts of major cities, at loading docks, around nuclear power plants, and in front of national icons such as the Brooklyn and Golden Gate Bridges. Few reservists anticipated that they were beginning a series of deployments that would in many cases last more than two years and put them for long stints in the midst of the wars in Afghanistan and Iraq.

In the immediate aftermath of 9/11, the U.S. Army first mobilized the 893rd MP Reserve Company for garrison duty at a military base in the western region of the States—known throughout this volume as Ft. McHenry—with the intent of freeing up professional military police personnel for overseas deployments. This first major deployment took place within a few weeks of the initial American invasion in Afghanistan and subsequent search for Osama bin Laden. The 893rd returned to the East Coast from this stateside deployment a year later, at about the same time the Bush administration was switching from diplomacy to an invasion of Iraq. By March 2003, when the U.S.

invaded Iraq, the 893rd was already training at a mobilization site for its inevitable deployment, and the company crossed the border from Kuwait heading north toward Baghdad within days of President Bush's announcement on board the USS *Abraham Lincoln* that the mission in Iraq had been "accomplished."

Like most Army Reserve units, the 893rd serves combat support functions, but its initial mission in Iraq was riddled with uncertainty. Even as the soldiers traveled from their stateside mobilization base through their initial crossing into Iraq, the company had been reassigned missions several times over. The 893rd ultimately was ordered to convoy north and help run a makeshift enemy prisoner of war camp outside of Baghdad. Fortunately for the company, its service in Iraq occurred during the early stages of the war, a period of relative goodwill among the Iraqi people. While mortar attacks, roadside improvised explosive devises, and prisoner uprisings were constant threats, the deadliest of insurgent attacks did not arise until after the company returned home.[4] The members of the 893rd take as a point of relief and pride that they returned from Iraq a fully intact unit. While several of their sister companies within the battalion suffered casualties during this period of service, the members of the 893rd sustained only a few minor injuries. They came home to the States in the winter of 2003 to a heroes' welcome that would soon be tarnished by the shocking images of the military police abuses at Abu Ghraib prison, which hit the news in April 2004. While this unit did not serve at the now infamous prison, many returning military police reservists, including members of the 893rd, found themselves questioned about their assignments by civilian friends, family members, and acquaintances.

In retrospect, while the jolt, anger, and patriotism generated by 9/11 propelled many of the members of the 893rd unhesitatingly to accept or even to volunteer for the initial call to duty, they were ultimately unprepared for the reality of being an integral component of fighting the wars in Afghanistan and Iraq. Even reservists with considerable experience were shocked by the length of their deployments and time away from home. Looking back on their deployments, Jeremy Easton, a sergeant (noncommissioned officer) with eight years of professional soldiering in the active component under his belt plus six years in the reserves, reflects the sentiments of many:

> One year was rough [in Iraq]. We did it, so I guess a year is feasible. But you've got guys goin' out now that are looking at eighteen months and twenty-four months. That's just too much. That's too much to ask somebody who's got a whole other life to take care of, so. It's one thing when you join and that's your sole purpose on the active component. You know that's what's expected of you, so you don't really have any place to complain. But even in the reserve component, you kinda expect, you kinda know you have an obligation, or you should know that you have an obligation, but I don't think anybody was ready for—I know that nobody in this company was ready for what we got hit with the last two years.

Now settling back into his civilian life and looking forward to spending as much time as possible with his wife and toddler daughter, Jeremy expresses his strong desire to be "free and clear" of the army. Given that he had only two more months on his military contract at the time of our conversation, he was gone from the 893rd by the fall of 2004. Unlike his colleagues who remain under contractual obligation to the Army Reserve, Jeremy has no further possibility of future deployments.

Their Life Stories

All of the reservists we came to know told unique stories about their lives before, during, and after their post-9/11 deployments. Still, experiencing these conversations and poring over their transcripts revealed that some reservists' stories adhere closely to one another. Finding these clusters of individuals is substantially a bottom-up process of interpretation in which some reservists appear to have life stories that parallel one another while at the same time diverging significantly from the life stories of other colleagues in the same company, under the same command, and performing the same military missions. The accounts they render about their lives are neither a potpourri of individual stories nor a singular metastory of citizen-soldiering. Instead, their life histories reveal three distinctive clusters of citizen-soldiers who have traveled similar paths.[5]

Adaptive Reservists

All of the reservists carry imprints from their nearly two years of back-to-back deployments and service in a war with no clear lines between the combat zone and rearguard safe havens. Still, one cluster, adaptive reservists, adjusts quickly, moving lockstep with changing institutional expectations as a result of a dynamic sense of their identity and of relational networks that run deep at home and in the military. These reservists cut across gender groups to include men who have experienced international deployments as well as all of the female reservists who had been raised in military families.[6]

Craig McCormick is an adaptive reservist whose commitment to the military began about twenty years ago when he joined the regular, all-volunteer army out of high school. Craig speaks with a quick cadence and embodies the perfect military carriage, shoulders squared and head held high, displaying a confidence in both his posture and his voice. After serving out his standard contract as a soldier and earning his discharge, Craig attended college and began a career in speech therapy. Along the way to his civilian career, Craig married, and he and his wife, Jill, had several children in quick succession. Despite his satisfaction with family life, Craig still desired a more exhilarating career in a field such as criminal justice. Now that he was a family man with deep community ties, Craig's needs were not the only ones to be considered when seeking a career shift. Rather than disrupt his "nice civilian life" of marriage, fatherhood, and rich community and extended-family ties, Craig settled on returning to the military in the MP Reserve Corps about a year prior to 9/11 and keeping his secure job at a university. Craig recalls a conversation with his wife about entering the reserves:

> And of course, before I [reenlisted], my wife and I talked about what it's going to mean to go back in the reserves, and then we were thinking the one weekend a month and the summer—"Yeah, but it

shouldn't be too bad. Of course, if anything ever does happen, then I would have to go, okay." But at that point, it's a remote possibility.

When we spoke with him following his deployments, Craig, now approaching his forties, was attempting to balance his desire to become an officer in the all-volunteer, professional army with his desire to satisfy his wife's strong wish to get their civilian lives back to normal. While Jill is comfortable with being married to a citizen-soldier and proudly made the required sacrifices to keep the family running smoothly during Craig's two extended deployments, she is much less comfortable subjecting their children to the rigors of regular military life. The geographic mobility required of professional military families could take its toll on their home environment, their church life, and their ability to assist their aging parents. Although as an officer, Craig is well positioned to transfer to the regular army, he is yielding to his family's needs and instead working his way up the Army Reserve ladder and maintaining his civilian position.

Struggling Reservists

American soldiers have been coming home from wars for more than two centuries with diverse experiences.[7] Still, the discovery of posttraumatic stress disorder following the Vietnam War provides a backdrop of veteran reentry that weighs most heavily on the contemporary American consciousness.[8] While some reservists from the 893rd tell stories of the stresses of war, many members of the group we call struggling reservists reveal troubles that are more a product of homegrown circumstances than experiences specific to serving in a war zone.[9] The 893rd was deployed involuntarily with limited warning and no concrete information about the nature of its deployment, including length, location, or specific missions. Not all families and reservists are equally equipped to handle such disruptions, and both reservists and their family members already living under stressed conditions found the deployments particularly difficult to navigate. Unreasonable expectations flowed in both directions as family members wanted more involvement by deployed reservists and the reservists wanted unyielding support from family members struggling to keep things together in their absence. Many of the reservists throw themselves completely into their deployments and block out their homegrown troubles, at least temporarily. Most of the reservists within this grouping occupy the lower rungs of the American workforce and have little education beyond high school. While the majority of the struggling soldiers are men who express their views about war and relationships in masculine terms, Michelle Colton's experiences also illustrate the difficulties struggling soldiers face.

Michelle comes across as a bit of a tomboy, and with her short bobbed hair styled within military regulations, it is easy to mistake her for someone still in her mid-teens rather than a young woman of twenty-two. However, engaging Michelle in conversation reveals someone with experiences and responsibilities of a mature woman well beyond her age. Prior to 9/11, Michelle was already struggling to make her way in the world, and the deployments ironically provided her temporary relief from incredible household responsibilities.

> In my household, it's only me, my mom, and my grandmother. And I basically have all the responsibility for them. Me and my mom share the responsibility of taking care of my grandmother, but I feel that I'm the mom sometimes, so that when I left, my mom actually had to take responsibility. She used to just go to work, come home, go to sleep, wake up, go to work. It was easy for her, and I was trying to go to school at one point, and full-time job, come home do all that, and she never had to worry about it. But as soon as I was deployed for the first time, it was a big shock to her, and the first deployment was pretty rough. . . . She didn't take that first deployment well at all. The responsibility she took on, she started getting angry, because she was like, "I don't want to do this," or she was getting frustrated with my grandmother. My grandmother didn't show her appreciation, and I was like, "Now you see what I went through while I was there." She couldn't handle it. She wasn't used to me not being around, and I had to get home on an emergency leave because she let the stress get to her too much, and she tried to do something crazy. So I had to go back there and smooth everything out again, and I remember I wasn't going to come back from Ft. McHenry. I was going to transfer and stay at

Ft. McHenry because I loved it there so much, and it was I just didn't want to come back to *that* either.

Despite wanting to stay in the Ft. McHenry area and establish a new life for herself, Michelle returned home and was dismayed by what she found.

When I came back, I noticed the house was a wreck. I was like "Ah, no. No. No." I'm back now, and I was trying to clean up, and I was getting frustrated and she was getting frustrated with me. And I was like, "Look, I love the Ft. McHenry area a lot. I think I'm going to go ahead and move there." Got some jobs lined up, and I had a place to go. Everything was just perfect. She gave me a couple of problems with that.

She was just getting adjusted to the medication she was on, so that was like a roller-coaster for me, and just getting back in the groove of things, because the whole routine at the house changed. I was still stateside and it changed like that. . . . My routine, the house gets cleaned. You eat something, you clean it up. You put it away, and I'm coming back and my mom just left an empty can here and a paper plate. I mean, a paper plate—just throw it in a trash can. My mom picked up old habits. Simple things, just—when the animals got fed. My mom would feed them whenever they were hungry, and I come back and my cat looks like a meatball. I'm like, "Wow, we don't need a Garfield or something. They get fed in the morning and maybe at night, not every four hours." . . . It ended up getting smoothed over, but it took a long time.

Oddly enough, the Iraq deployment was easier for Michelle's family to handle, and after she completed this second tour, she returned home to resume her responsibilities as caregiver to her grandmother, the primary support system for her mother, and an assistant in a veterinarian's hospital.

That she joined the Reserve as a teenager and was soon involuntarily deployed for just under two years, including nearly a year as a guard in a decrepit and dangerous prison outside of Baghdad, is not to say that Michelle's life has been ruined by this experience. The deployments enabled her to gain respect within and independence from her family while acquiring skills and status to better position herself in a job market with limited opportunities for people whose only academic credential is a high school diploma. At the same time, the deployments added further strain to her caregiving arrangements with her mother and grandmother as well as hurt her immediate financial situation, forcing her to lose a car and undermining her standing as an American consumer with good credit. Michelle is keenly aware of this duality of deployment benefits and costs as she explains,

> It takes a toll on working because I'm just getting to know my [civilian] job and they're getting to know me, and now I'm gone, and I got to come back and relearn the whole thing. It's a pain sometimes, but it's got a lot of benefits, too, so people at work are, "So you're in the reserves?" And it just helps me gain position in a lot of jobs, too.

Resistant Reservists

A third cluster, which we call resistant reservists, consists of those who resent the interruption of their civilian routines, dismiss military life while they live it, and are more likely to oppose the war even as they fight in it. Resistant reservists are males with high civilian expectations and college anticipated or already a part of their lives. Their stories are much like that of Travis Shaffer, who like many young men and women trying to figure out how to pay for college, began his service in the Army Reserve straight out of high school and planned to make good use of the military's educational benefits.

Travis has a clean-cut, boy-next-door look and gives the impression that he would be much more comfortable in a baseball cap, jeans, and a t-shirt than the BDUs he wears when we see him. When he grows anxious in telling about the strains of being deployed so rapidly following 9/11 or the repeated calls to service, an ever-so-slight lisp works its way into his speech. Although he felt a strong desire to serve his country, Travis never really envisioned the role of reservists extending much beyond the standard one weekend a month and two weeks a year training commitment. He could work his college courses around that schedule and finish his bachelor's degree in a timely fashion; however, this plan took a sharp detour. As an East Coast MP reservist, his first call to service occurred within hours of the 9/11 attacks, when his former company was called to help with heightened security.

> On September 11, I was in class, and I remember what happened, and honest to God, after I realized no one was joking, I saw [the Twin Towers coming down] on TV, instantly—I mean, instantly—I knew I was gonna go somewhere. And from that moment on, all I could do was sit around and think about when are they going to call, when are they going to call? Ironically, it was only three hours later. . . . But now [having come home from multiple deployments], I think about it all the time. Oh my gosh, it's just the worst, cause the army cannot give you any kind of concrete answer on whether or not you can go again or what the time frame is now that we've done two years.

This initial deployment lasted no more than two weeks, but it foreshadowed the changes about to take place in his life. Soon after returning to college and making up his missed course work, Travis learned that he and several other close friends from his platoon were being involuntarily transferred to a different MP company within the same battalion that was gearing up for an extended deployment. With the United States having just invaded Afghanistan in search of Osama bin Laden and having transported presumed members of al-Qaeda to the American military base at Guantanamo Bay, Cuba, Travis—and most of the soldiers we interviewed from the 893rd—assumed that this call would mean they were shipping off to either Afghanistan or Cuba. To his relief, the 893rd was instead assigned garrison duty at Ft. McHenry, a base near a thriving city in the western United States. At least for the time being, they would serve stateside. After a short stint at home, during which he resumed college, Travis was devastated to learn in a few months that he would be pulled away from another semester of college, this time for Iraq. Travis never fully embraced military ideology and fights to maintain his individuality in an institution that demands conformity.

> I have a citizen mentality even in the military. When I joined the military, yes, they try to make you a drone, make you a robot, and, I mean,

there are—to some extent, that stuff is good, you know—in a life-and-death situation, I'm sure it would work. But when it comes to conversation and problem solving, I use my civilian side all the time. . . . I was a civilian in the army. Yes, they call me a soldier, but as a reservist, reservists are civilians in the army, because you have a lot more common sense than an active-duty soldier by far. . . . You can think for yourself. You can follow instructions; maybe one of the downsides as a reservist is you're prone to question things more often. You're prone to question authority, but that's only because the rest of your life as a civilian, that's what you do. You're allowed to question authority, you know, and you're allowed to make your own decisions, and you're not told or bossed. But I—definitely, I'm a civilian in the army.

With civilian life interrupted for three deployments over the span of two years, Travis struggled to keep his relationship with his girlfriend intact. Still, they broke up several weeks following our conversation with him. Travis now bitterly distrusts the military organization that he views as causing such great interruptions to his civilian life. He has never supported the war in Iraq and notes,

If you were talking about ultimate sacrifice, I mean, I totally think that, like, people, you know, who died over there, I don't want to say they died in vain, but I think it's sad that they did die. I mean it's not the Civil War, Revolutionary War, you know, World War II—I mean, you knew what you were dying for, and the whole world said of you they loved you for dying for it, you know. It's not that way, it's not that way, and no, if I would have died, I probably would have had to come back and haunt somebody. I would have been pissed off.

When we spoke with him in the spring of 2004, he was back in college for the third time and living in constant fear and uncertainty that the military, stretched thin in Iraq and Afghanistan, could call him and the company to active duty again, presuming, "If you do go again, you're gonna go back overseas."

Travis Shaffer is among a small group of reservists from the 893rd who clearly resist the army's ways and who are angry about the demands placed on them after 9/11. At the same time, nearly all of the reservists distrust any promises made about their future in the military. None expresses a desire to go back to Iraq, particularly after having been home for six months. They feel that two years of back-to-back deployments, including nearly a year in Iraq, fulfills their "contracts" with the military with regard to being called up and deployed. In fact, the authority that President Bush invoked to call up the Reserve (and the National Guard) after 9/11 dates back to the end of the Vietnam War and allows reservists to be deployed an unlimited number of times as long as no single deployment is longer than twenty-four consecutive months. The Pentagon, not the presidential order, has interpreted the post-9/11 call-up as twenty-four cumulative months, and the reservists are banking on this interpretation to keep them home for the duration of the Iraq and Afghanistan Wars. The Pentagon is continuously revisiting this unofficial policy, given that it was formulated when no military planners thought America would be fighting two foreign wars for more than four years.[10] The policy that grew out of the end of the draft after the Vietnam War coupled with the reality of the shifting nature of reservists' "contracts" with the U.S. Army have left even the most resilient of the citizen-soldiers we met adrift in a sea of uncertainty. Struggling and resistant reservists voice even stronger sentiments of distrust and resentment toward the military. Their lives are no longer their own. The nearly fifty years of the Reserve as the home of America's weekend warriors has come to an abrupt end. They are now the new conscripts of the twenty-first-century U.S. Army.

one

Shadows of Vietnam

"We Ought to Call Up the Reserves"

Military commanders returning from America's defeat in the Vietnam War vowed that they would never again send the U.S. Army into sustained combat without calling up reserve forces. They made good on this promise and in doing so set the stage for what has ultimately led to more than 186,000 reserve soldiers, including the 893rd Military Police Reserve Company, being deployed in the wars of Afghanistan and Iraq after 9/11.[1] According to General Earl G. Wheeler, former chairman of the Joint Chiefs of Staff,

> We felt that it would be desirable to have a reserve call-up in order to make sure that the people of the U.S. knew that we were in a war and not engaged at some two-penny military adventure. Because we didn't think it was going to prove to be a two-penny military adventure by any manner or means.[2]

In the early months of 1965, U.S. executive and military leaders agreed that the Vietnam War was going badly. In early January, elite elements of the South Vietnamese Army were defeated by the Vietcong in major battles, North Vietnamese Army units were beginning to move into

South Vietnam, and there was deep concern that the North was preparing for an all-out offensive on Saigon (now Ho Chi Min City), the capital of South Vietnam. In the words of Robert McNamara, then secretary of defense, "South Vietnam seemed to be on the brink of total collapse."[3] On January 27, McNamara and his deputy, McGeorge Bundy, met with President Lyndon Johnson to discuss what became known as the "fork in the road" memorandum, which said that to avoid defeat, the president needed to decide between a major escalation of U.S. military power in Vietnam or an all-out effort to negotiate as favorable a withdrawal as possible given the conditions on the ground. McNamara and Bundy favored escalation while making sure the president knew that his secretary of state, Dean Rusk, wanted to find a way to make the existing course of aid and military assistance to the South Vietnamese government work because he saw no favorable consequences resulting from either escalation or withdrawal.

Johnson decided on escalation, accepting recommendations from the civilian and military leaders of the Defense Department to initiate bombing of North Vietnam and commit U.S. ground forces to wage war in South Vietnam. He increased troop strength from 23,000 to 175,000 in 1965 with the knowledge that the Pentagon wanted an additional 100,000 men committed in 1966. The debate shifted to how such a force would be put together and deployed—specifically, whether to call up reserve forces.[4] At a July 13, 1965, press conference, President Johnson floated the possibility of mobilizing the Reserve: "Any substantial increase in the present level of our efforts to turn back the aggressors in South Vietnam will require steps to insure that our reserves of men and equipment of the United States remain entirely adequate for any and all emergencies."[5] And, in a July 14 phone conversation with McNamara, the president seemed to be leaning toward calling up the Reserve, a decision strongly favored by the Pentagon's civilian and military leaders.

> **McNamara:** If we do go as far as my paper suggested—sending numbers of men over there—we ought to call up the reserves. . . . Almost surely, if we called up reserves, you would want to go to the Congress to get additional authority. This would be a vehicle for draw-

ing together support. Now you'd say, "Along with that approach [escalation], we are . . . continuing this political initiative to probe for a willingness to negotiate a reasonable settlement here. And we ask your support under these circumstances." And that's a vehicle by which you both get the authority to call up the reserves and also tie them into the whole program.

President: Well, that makes sense.[6]

On July 21, the president polled the defense and military leaders on his National Security Council, securing unanimity for escalation that included mobilization of reserve forces. However, at a National Security Council meeting one week later, Johnson indicated that he did not favor going to Congress for everything the White House and Pentagon might desire, including declaring a state of emergency and calling up the reserves. Instead, he added another option, proposing to give the military what it wanted but avoiding a call-up of reserves. The president again polled the room regarding his revised option to escalate without going to Congress or mobilizing the Reserve. The key moment came when the president turned to General Earl Wheeler, the chairman of the Joint Chiefs of Staff:

> "Do you, General Wheeler, agree?" Wheeler nodded his agreement. It was said, by someone who was present, an extraordinary moment, like watching a lion-tamer dealing with some of the great lions. Everyone knew that Wheeler objected, that the Chiefs wanted more, that they wanted a wartime footing and a call-up of the Reserves; the thing they feared most was a partial war and a partial commitment.[7]

Wheeler and the rest of the Pentagon were planning to escalate initially with a partial call-up of 235,000 reserve forces, believing that the Reserve was crucial to securing an effective fighting force and generating the needed popular support for prosecuting what everyone in the room presumed would be a long war. According to at least one insider, General John A. Wickham, the sentiments were so strong in the Pentagon about calling up the Reserve that the Joint Chiefs talked about resignation when the initial decision was made to delay the mobilization of reserve forces.

In 1964–66, I served as military assistant to Army Chief of Staff Harold K. Johnson and recall many deliberations of the Joint Chiefs of Staff and army leaders about the need to call up reserves for Vietnam. General Johnson and the other chiefs made their case with the president, who decided against any call-up. The Joint Chiefs debated among themselves whether to resign as a result of their disagreements with the president, but they decided that the more prudent and appropriate course would be to continue serving and do what was possible to support the war without a call-up of reserves.[8]

Despite top military advisers' repeated requests to mobilize the Reserve, on July 28 the president announced plans to increase U.S. forces immediately to 125,000, deciding that the buildup would be secured through increased conscription. Without mobilizing the Reserve, the president could continue to pursue his very ambitious social agenda and escalate "without exposing the depth of U.S. involvement" in Vietnam.[9] The Pentagon tried again in 1966 and 1967 to persuade the president to call up the Reserve, but to no avail. Both the White House and the Pentagon recognized the Reserve's political significance to any war effort. President Johnson realized that a call-up of the reserves would "require a great deal of money and a huge sacrifice for the American people."[10] He recalled the domestic political turmoil that arose when President John F. Kennedy had mobilized the reserves during the 1961 Berlin crisis: after he floated the idea of calling up the Reserve, members of Congress reported that they were already getting flak from families who would likely be affected were the reserves mobilized. The political calculations of Johnson and Congress converged as most politicians saw fewer obstacles to expanding the draft than to mobilizing reserve forces. Two analysts of these events put the political calculations in stark terms: "Reservists and guardsmen were better connected, better educated, more affluent, and whiter than their peers in the active forces."[11]

Whether or not these factors drove the political decision to withhold the reserve, historians broadly agree that the question of mobilizing the Reserve was a major policy issue carried on inside the U.S. government from 1965 through 1967 with little public awareness or debate.[12] For the

Pentagon, the president's decision meant that the manpower to wage a ground war in Vietnam would rely on conscripts and inexperienced officers and that the best opportunity for securing public support for what was rapidly becoming an American war was lost.

> Failure to call up reserves meant that the army, for example, had to expand from roughly 900K to over 1.5 million by rapid training and promotion of conscripts and officers. As a result, we fought the early years of the Vietnam War with less experienced junior leaders than we might have had were the Guard and reservists called up. Consequently, we might have suffered fewer casualties and achieved more tactical successes if the army had been able to expand with experienced NCOs [noncommissioned officers] and officers from the Guard and reserves. Moreover, a call-up would have engaged the public more closely with the war effort, thus engendering more public support.[13]

An added consequence of the president's decision was that the Reserve as an institution was "ripped" apart.[14] The established members of the Reserve, particularly its NCOs and officers, were veterans of the active military and previous military campaigns. While these reservists were not anxious to go to war, they had strong ties to the military and substantial experience to draw upon when deployed to war zones. With the president's decision to withhold these forces, the Reserve became a refuge for the disaffected and a haven for those whose connections allowed them to avoid the draft. Divided internally and withheld from the battlefield, the Reserve's public image plummeted, and a critical link between the military and civilian spheres of American life was severed.

Total Force Policy

The individual who received the initial assignment to mobilize U.S. Army forces for the escalation of the Vietnam War without the Reserve was a legendary soldier, General Creighton Abrams. He also put in motion the policy that would restore the reputation of the Reserve and determine its fate to be a force deployed en masse to Afghanistan and Iraq after 9/11. Already a highly decorated combat commander, Abrams broke into the public consciousness in the winter of 1944 when the German army launched its last counteroffensive of World War II in the Ardennes, a plateau region of France. Elements of U.S. forces, including the 101st Airborne Division, were trapped in the town of Bastogne. Colonel Abrams led the 37th Tank Battalion of the U.S. Army, which broke through enemy lines, rescuing the American troops from certain defeat and playing a crucial role in halting the German army's last great offensive operation in Europe.[15] He went on to command forces in the Korean War and in Europe during the 1950s and early 1960s. In 1964, General Abrams was promoted to army vice chief of staff; at the Pentagon, he oversaw the buildup of U.S. Army forces in Vietnam during the period of rapid escalation and commitment of American combat ground forces between 1965 and 1967. While he took pride in his job of strengthening the army under crisis conditions, Abrams felt that America had entered a war unprepared and failed to employ what he initially referred to as "one army" preparedness and later as "total force doctrine."

> Our arrangement was that we would have one Army with certain things in the active force, others in the National Guard, and yet others in the Army Reserve. And if the unfortunate circumstance should occur that . . . we'd have to use the Army [then we would] use the active, the National Guard and the Reserve together. That's the only way [we would] do it. So all the maintenance, all of the supply, a lot of the medical—all of those things we've got to have, they're the reserve. . . . But somehow it didn't quite work out that way. Instead we [used] the Army in Vietnam *minus* the National Guard and the Army Reserve.[16]

After overseeing the buildup of the army to implement the president's decision to escalate American involvement in Vietnam and a five-year tour of duty in Vietnam, Abrams returned to Washington, D.C., in October 1972 as the army's chief of staff. One of his first assignments was to conduct a phased withdrawal of American troops from Vietnam. With the war ending in defeat and the draft terminated in 1973, Abrams reflected on the Vietnam experience and was in a position of power to act on his reflections. The Vietnam War reinforced his long-standing concerns about America's strong tendency to go to war unprepared: "I can't help but be appalled at the human costs we've paid. . . . We've had to put [forces] together under the strain of emergency, and we've had to have relatively untrained men, led by relatively untrained men, do a very difficult task."[17] The move to an all-volunteer army that relies substantially on a combat force of professional, active-duty soldiers would go a long way toward correcting this problem, assuming that the force was robust enough to meet civilian leaders' many demands on the military. However, Abrams had an additional concern that was far more politically delicate, given the axiom of American governance that ultimate authority over the military, including whether, when, and under what circumstances the United States will send troops into combat, rests with elected civilian authorities. Abrams, like many of his contemporaries, was deeply disturbed that President Johnson had decided to tiptoe America into the Vietnam War without the public's full awareness and commitment. He saw soldiers perform bravely and consistently under battlefield conditions but also witnessed growing difficulties he attributed to a reliance on conscription without public backing. He, like many of his contemporaries, witnessed defeat and the "explosive problems of dissent, drugs, racism and indiscipline" that became the army's defining features as the war ground to a halt.[18]

Based on their reflections on Vietnam, Abrams and his contemporaries regarded the mobilization of reserve forces as the crucial decision that must be taken any time America was contemplating engagement of its military in sustained combat. These leaders reasoned that failure to do so in Vietnam meant that escalation occurred without full public awareness and undermined public commitment to the war. One analyst of Abrams's moves to reconfigure military preparedness and force structure in the 1970s says that the general "believed that the liberal use of reserve forces in future conflicts would cause the American people to more quickly validate long-term and large-scale use of military forces. If validation was not forthcoming, one outcome would be fewer casualties and lower overall cost, with the emphasis on the former."[19] While Abrams never publicly spoke about his intention to build a force structure that would check civilian authorities, there is little doubt that he intended to do so.[20] General John Vessey, who worked closely with Abrams during this period, recalls Abrams saying that America would never again deploy a significant force without the mobilization of reserve forces and that by doing so, the armed forces would be restored as an "expression of the nation."[21] Lewis Sorley, General Abrams's biographer, interviewed James Schlesinger, who served as secretary of defense when Abrams was reformulating the army's force structure:

> "There is no question but that Abrams was deliberately integrating reserve and active forces in that manner," said James Schlesinger. [Sorley asked,] "Did that constitute a forcing function?" Schlesinger puffed his pipe, considering. "That would really not be like Abe," he said. "He had the view that the military must defer to the civilians, even to an extraordinary degree. I speculate that the military sought to fix the incentives so that the civilians would act appropriately."[22]

Schlesinger endorsed Abrams's plan to build a "total force" army that would initially have sixteen combat divisions, thirteen of active-duty forces and three "rounding out" divisions of highly trained National Guard combat units. Any support forces needed to maintain the army in the field for sustained combat, including medics, cargo handlers, maintenance and transportation personnel, and military police, would largely be the responsibility of the Reserve. Total force—commonly referred to as the Abrams Doctrine—became formal policy in 1973 when the general issued a letter to the U.S. Army's thirteen field commanders. Abrams said that the army would move to a force structure of sixteen combat-ready divisions by 1978 and simultaneously bolster "the readiness and responsiveness of the Reserve Components, integrating them fully into the total force."[23] Abrams died less than a month later, but his vision of the army remained the guiding principle for revitalizing its fighting capacity and public image.

Reserve Buildup and Readiness

Given the reserve forces' low prestige in the eyes of the regular military after Vietnam and the sorry state of the reserves' preparedness, the transition to total force practice was rocky in its formative years and was never fully tested until after 9/11. By the end of the 1970s, reserve units' readiness fell well below military standards.[24] In October 1978, a secret Pentagon worldwide deployment exercise known as Nifty Nugget showed serious deficiencies not only in the number of trained reserve forces but in the logistics of pulling these reservists from their civilian-sector occupations.[25]

During the 1980s, the Reagan administration launched the largest peacetime military buildup in U.S. history and rapidly expanded the amount of resources and number of personnel in both the active-duty and reserve components of the armed forces. By the end of the 1980s, military reservists and National Guardsmen constituted half of all trained military personnel.[26] A dramatic increase also occurred between 1980 and 1986 in the total number of reserve forces available for presidential call-ups. As the total force policy was put into place, the law initially limited the availability of reserve troops to fifty thousand personnel accessible under a presidential mobilization, but this would not last long. In 1980, President Jimmy Carter doubled that number, and in 1986 President Ronald Reagan doubled it again.[27] Consequently, as President George H. W. Bush entered the period of Desert Storm, or the first Gulf War in 1990, he had at his disposal up to two hundred thousand reservists who could be mobilized without the declaration of a national emergency.[28]

But the Reserve and National Guard suffered a major setback in 1990–91 when President Bush decided to exclude the highly trained and motivated Army Reserve combat units from missions in Iraq, opting instead to mobilize fifty thousand combat support units.[29] This time, military leaders did not want the combat reserves, arguing that they were not fully ready.[30] Siding with the military leadership, Defense Secretary Dick Cheney stated the position of the first Bush administration: "The Guard and Reserve provide a very significant component for our military capacity . . . but I'm not eager to send units that aren't fully ready."[31] In a turnabout from the Vietnam War, reserve components and some congressional leaders lobbied Cheney to send reserve force combat units to the Middle East in support of Operation Desert Storm/Desert Shield.[32]

With the brevity of the Gulf War, the army's reluctance to deploy combat units, and the fact that most combat support units operated safely behind the lines of battle,[33] the U.S. military response to 9/11 turned out to be the first real-time test of the total force policy as both a military and a political manpower issue. The wars in Afghanistan and Iraq have required extended deployments of reserve combat and combat support forces, including the call-up of the 893rd Military Police Company. Along with professional soldiers, members of the Reserve and National Guard bear the burden of sacrifice for homeland security, the Iraq War, and the Afghanistan War. While most Americans continue life as normal, catching glimpses of the wars on the TV evening news, the lives of the citizen-soldiers have been taken over by total force policy.

two

Deploying the 893rd MP Company

"Do You Know Where the Fuck We Are?!?"

It's like when I first got in country, they needed someone to do a [prisoner hospital transfer] mission, and . . . a truck had exploded right in front of me. And it's really hard to not think about. It's like ten feet in front of you. That's when everything starts running through your mind like, "What's going on? Now it's really happening." You're really there, and if something were to happen, you couldn't really help it. It's just happening. And it was just the most terrifying thing I've ever been through, and I never wanted to leave [the prison camp] again. I never wanted to volunteer for a mission, and with everything else, that's the fear that you have, and you eventually get over that fear, but it's the initial fear right away that, you know, gets you and the fact that the prisoner that I had—which was one of the top ten most wanted criminals in Iraq—that it could have been meant for me, and they missed and they got the wrong one. And it was just the scariest thing I've ever been through and the biggest experience that I will never forget.

—Enlisted Army Reservist Jeff Temple

When the 9/11 attacks took place, Jeff Temple was barely out of high school and had only recently finished his advanced individual training as part of his enlistment in the Army Reserve. Less than two years later, Jeff and the rest of the 893rd MP Company were deployed to Iraq, having already completed nearly a yearlong deployment in the States. Jeff had thrived during the 893rd's stateside garrison deployment, finding the work, the location, the excitement, and the income far superior to anything in his rural hometown community. With no war-zone experience but a lot of media exposure that gave him a glorified imagination of what it meant to be a soldier in combat, he eagerly volunteered for a prisoner transfer mission soon after arriving at a makeshift prison just outside of Baghdad. In response to encountering the life-and-death situation that he will never forget, he retreated back to the somewhat safer confines of the prison camp, realizing that he was no longer a military reservist working a stateside deployment of checking IDs and running patrol, as he had dreamed when he enlisted. With boots on the ground in Iraq, Jeff was awakened to the harsh realities of the random quality of injury and death associated with being a soldier in a war zone with no delineated boundaries.

War-zone deployments are a central focus of both military history and wartime chronicles written by and about soldiers.[1] The narratives of the reservists of the 893rd are consistent with their claims that war prompts soldiers to concentrate on "the job," or the importance of performing tasks with a full awareness that the only way to affect the surrounding danger is to work together.[2] Bonds among soldiers are strongly featured in these accounts and are associated with their mutual dependency for security as well as the shared experiences of adventure, danger, and seeing carnage every day. Such "bonds of brotherhood" are evident in many of the narratives of the 893rd, particularly as the reservists chronicle moments of their lives together in Baghdad under conditions of extreme danger. However, the convergence of some soldiers' stories with typified representations of soldiering in times of war does not capture the whole story of being a part of the 893rd, particularly when their accounts are examined closely and with an eye to the influence of time and the likelihood that bonding is as much about boundary setting as about brotherhood.

Deployments of the 893rd

The Gulf War of 1990–91 marked a point in time when total force policy was both undermined and put to use. The Army National Guard combat brigades that trained to go into the battlefield with active-duty combat forces were not deployed to expel the Iraqi military from Kuwait.[3] At the same time, nearly fifty thousand army reservists who served in military support positions were activated, and many of these reservists were deployed to the Persian Gulf. The deployment of support units included military police whose soldiers set up and maintained detention facilities to house prisoners of war, mostly in remote parts of Saudi Arabia.[4]

The 893rd existed only on paper at the time of the Gulf War, having been decommissioned after World War II. The period immediately following the Gulf War marked a reduction in funding for Army Reserve and National Guard forces. However, the 893rd bucked this trend and was reinstated during the mid-1990s as a consequence of the growing demand for military police reserve units. While the Gulf War, for example, lasted only about one hundred hours, it produced seventy thousand enemy prisoners of war.[5] Many individuals who filled the ranks of the 893rd during the 1990s were formerly active-duty soldiers or long-term reservists who served voluntarily in other MP units that were deployed to quick wars, like the invasion of Panama, and peacemaking missions, including NATO operations in the Balkan states. Still, the 893rd as a unit had not been deployed since World War II. That is, not until after 9/11.

Winding Up for Stateside Deployment

On September 15, 2001, President George W. Bush authorized Operation Noble Eagle, the within borders or "homeland" security operation assigned to the military immediately after 9/11. The U.S. military thus began mobilizing hundreds of reserve units, including the 893rd. Senior commissioned and noncommissioned officers of the unit, unlike many of the low-ranking enlistees such as specialists, were not at all surprised that they were among the first units to be mobilized, since the 893rd is designated a "tier 1" unit, ready for active deployment as a result of its combination of personnel, equipment, and training. With no known destination in sight, the 893rd began preparations for a full deployment scheduled to commence within a few short weeks.

Despite their designation as tier 1 prepared, the 893rd lacked adequate personnel for rapid deployment. As a result, many individuals were involuntarily transferred from other units to the 893rd, and still others, wanting to be useful in the aftermath of the World Trade Center and Pentagon destruction, came to the unit as individual volunteers in search of immediate deployment. Some of the involuntary transfers had served very brief deployments just after 9/11, with responsibilities including securing military sites close to their home reserve centers or the crash site of United Airlines flight 93, the fourth hijacked plane that crashed in a rural area southeast of Pittsburgh, Pennsylvania. Military policy indicates that reservists should be ready at all times to deploy within seventy-two hours for a full deployment. While existing members of the 893rd tended to have upward of three weeks to ready themselves for their transition from civilian to soldier life, reservists who were transferring into the company had only a couple of days or even hours to put their civilian lives in order and report for duty. Travis Shaffer, the young college student featured in the introduction, had already left school the day after 9/11 to serve an immediate and brief security deployment, and by late September 2001, he was among about a dozen soldiers involuntarily transferred from a sister MP company to the 893rd. Travis was one of the last soldiers called to help fill out the unit's ranks, receiving an extremely brief notification: "They called in the afternoon and said, 'Can you be here tomorrow morning?'" As a single college student, Travis had a somewhat simple web of civilian matters to attend to before leaving town, compared to other members of the 893rd, who have multiple dependents and demanding jobs. Still, he had to withdraw from school, sell his books, organize his bank accounts for direct withdrawal of bills, establish power of attorney, and arrange to move out of the apartment where he had been living with his girlfriend.

In the early fall of 2001, the 893rd packed up and shipped out to Ft. McHenry, a military base in the western United States. Even for those reservists who received more notice, the time leading up to the departure was punctuated by only vague references to the location, length, and mission of their impending deployment. Jorge Mercado, a more senior-ranking member of the company, leans back and gives a nervous laugh as he recalls the disconnect between the certainty he felt in knowing that a deployment was imminent and the fuzziness of where they were going and what they would be doing:

> I called my parents and then said, "Hey, look, we're probably gonna end up going somewhere. I don't know where yet, but I'll let you know when I get there. I'll send you an e-mail or something." And my father was like, "Just be careful and keep us informed, and let us know your whereabouts," and stuff like that. So at the time, I had just gotten an apartment, and I had to get out of the lease, and so I called my best friend who lived pretty close to me, and I said, "Hey, look, I got like a week." I said, "I need you to pack all my stuff and throw it in storage."

Making preparations for the possibility of an Afghanistan deployment was a common response during this waiting period. Dennis Harris, a young enlistee recently transferred to the 893rd, was also among the many who packed with the expectation of ultimately heading to Afghanistan to provide support on that front. With his typical self-deprecating humor, Dennis laughs at himself as he recalls the initial packing:

> I'm thinkin' we're going to Afghanistan. I'm thinkin' like, "Holy crap!" I'm like—but it wasn't too big of an issue. It was just like it was a short notice, and I'm sittin' there tryin' to pack for as if I'm going to Afghanistan. All this shampoo, all this toothpaste, deodorant, soap, and everything, all this stuff, and then I finally find out we're going to Ft. McHenry. I'm like, "What do I need all this stuff for? They got stores at Ft. McHenry."

Mission Warp on First Deployment

Upon arriving at Ft. McHenry, the members of the company learned that they would augment the active-duty military police officers, already stationed at the base, who were working long hours to meet the demands of the increased security measures and to fill in the gaps of those active duty MPs who had already been shipped overseas. Nearly everyone in the 893rd, including senior officers, was surprised that their role in Operation Noble Eagle would be to augment the garrison duties, traditional police work on a military base, potentially for the next two years. Although reservist MPs receive training in all aspects of military police operations during the basic training and advanced individual training (AIT) that takes place on entering the reserves, once assigned to a particular company, they develop a military specialty. The 893rd had spent years training specifically to work enemy prisoner of war camps and were experts at setting up and guarding the perimeters of prisoner camps, referred to frequently as working "outside the wire." Many company members consequently were somewhat puzzled that in the midst of an international war, they were sent to run ID checks and patrol a military base on U.S. soil.

Some members found this mission generally frustrating, while others counted their blessings that they were not in the mountains of Afghanistan supporting combat units searching for Osama bin Laden or fighting the Taliban regime. All of them needed to shift gears into garrison work. For those reservists coming to the deployment from civilian police positions, this was a simple transition, and they provided much-needed training for their fellow company members. However, as Glenn Adams, a senior-level noncommissioned officer (NCO) with well over ten years of military-police-specific training, notes, "We pretty much had to learn from scratch down there." Jesse Barnes, whose law enforcement knowledge prior to this first deployment was primarily textbook-based through his college criminal justice courses, recollects being bewildered during his first days on the job:

> So we get down to Ft. McHenry, and we find we're doing this garrison mission, and we're like, "Wow, we haven't trained for this." And they go, "Here's your cruiser. Here's your gun. Go out and enforce, enforce the law." And I'm driving—I remember the first morning I'm driving out there, it's foggy. I didn't—I have no idea what's going on the base, and I can't see anything, and I was like, "I hope they don't call me or anything." But yeah, but actually we took classes, and we got educated in field sobriety tests, how to run a radar, utilizing your pepper spray, traffic stops, and we adjusted, and we did a good job down there. . . . And the thing about law enforcement training is that it just keeps going on and on. You keep learning new things every day. And I never felt fully . . . like a well-trained police officer.

Growing as a Company at Ft. McHenry

As their year of deployment at Ft. McHenry progressed, many soldiers grew comfortable with their military arrangements. Although a few civilian professionals struggled financially on military pay, college students and those at the shallow end of the civilian labor pool saved a lot of money because of deployment pay and base privileges. The ease of cell phone communication and airline travel enabled the soldiers to stay in close contact with girlfriends, boyfriends, fiancées, spouses, children, parents, close friends, and civilian employers. Those in partnerships encouraged family, friends, and lovers to visit when they had leave time, and a few even moved their entire families to apartments off base for the duration of their stateside deployment. Nearly all the members of the company traveled back to their hometowns to attend to everything from family health crises to weddings of friends and relatives.

As they learned to do police work by practicing it, the members of the 893rd began to appreciate the western U.S. city near the base. While initially surprised by their duties, many came to enjoy not only their geographic location but the garrison work of the military police. Garrett Wesner, a young man with limited worldly experience who enlisted in the reserves before departing high school, exemplifies this attitude when he enthusiastically recalls,

> The next thing I know, I'm in Ft. McHenry in a patrol car, which for me was great because I always wanted to be a cop, so I was having a blast. I was a ticket-writin' Nazi. And, I mean, it was fun for me. I mean, there's just no other way to put it. It was fun and then the city life. Hell, I'm a country boy, but you put me in a city for a year, I'll be happy. Then I would want to come back to the country.

The time spent together at Ft. McHenry enabled ties of friendship. During our conversational interviews, we ate lunch, or chow as we came to know it, with the senior officer and several senior-level NCOs of one of the platoons. Throughout lunch these men busted each other's chops as they recounted stories of their service together. Luis Balderas, a serious but fun-loving NCO, still gets teased about a high-speed chase at Ft. McHenry, noting, "I get heckled about it all the time because they say I secured him first, then I pepper foamed him." For many, Ft. McHenry was a time for cutting their teeth as active-duty soldiers. One reservist came home from this deployment with a new tattoo around his biceps commemorating the laceration he received while jumping a chain-link fence in pursuit of a suspect. Others took time on the base to grow in personal independence and sow wild oats. In the absence of disapproving parents, fiancées, or girlfriends, many of the men became skilled motorcyclists or took skydiving lessons that culminated in jumps.

Most members of the 893rd recognized that the deployment to Ft. McHenry, with its combination of training, working, and living together, moved the reservists in the direction of becoming a functioning company with greater trust in one another's capabilities and more rooted relationships with one another. While a handful of company members experienced financial, emotional, or relationship difficulties during their deployment to Ft. McHenry, it was a time for most reservists to shift gears from their civilian lives to more active soldier lives without the trauma of overseas deployment. As it would turn out, these strengthened relationships served them well when the conditions of their lives changed with their second deployment.

Transition to Iraq

After nearly a year of being mobilized and deployed to Ft. McHenry, the 893rd was sent home in the early fall of 2002. With just one year of deployment service now under their belts, they remained eligible for another year's worth of active duty, and as time drew near to head back home, rumors floated about the possibility of a second deployment, this time most likely overseas. When they did get home, company members quickly received even more suspicious clues to their future as they were told to get their soldier record programs in order, including child care plans, wills, and financial affairs. They also began a series of vaccinations, including anthrax vaccinations, to ward against biological agents of warfare. The U.S. pressure on Iraq was building momentum as the Bush administration increased its insistence that Saddam Hussein disclose the location of weapons of mass destruction. As international events unfolded, the members of the 893rd tried to reintegrate back to their routines of monthly drills, civilian jobs, college schedules, and family life. Some tried to remain in an alert soldier mind-set and readied their loved ones for the strong possibility of another extended deployment, while others lulled themselves into believing that one deployment would be enough to fulfill their military obligations.

While membership in the 893rd remained almost completely intact during the yearlong deployment to Ft. McHenry, the return home marked another period of reconstituting the unit. Some soldiers returned to their original companies, others retired completely from the military, and a few were promoted up and out of the company. One of the most seasoned soldiers' physical well-being was severely compromised by an overdose of the anthrax vaccination. New reserve recruits, fresh out of basic training, were assigned to the lower ranks, while other soldiers who had finished serving similar stateside MP deployments were involuntarily transferred to the 893rd to fill the remaining vacant spaces in anticipation of an overseas deployment.

About a month prior to the start of the U.S. invasion of Iraq, the reconstituted 893rd, like many other military police reserve companies, received mobilization orders for its second deployment. The time had come to ensure that they were properly geared up and trained for movement to Iraq. At the same time that the United States had begun its March 2003 missile strikes on Iraq, the members of the 893rd were hard at work at Ft. McGovern, a training facility in the southern United States. The captain of the 893rd issued orders prohibiting soldiers from going home during the training period and restricted severely the circumstances that would allow family members to visit Ft. McGovern. The military's grip on the lives of the reservists was clearly tightening beyond what had been the case at Ft. McHenry even as some of the enlisted soldiers snuck home when they had weekends off.

During their two and a half months at Ft. McGovern, the members of the 893rd received training across a spectrum of potential missions from escorting convoys to interning prisoners. As the weeks went by, the training focused more consistently on the latter, including the mission for which they had had the most training prior to 9/11—working outside the wire of prison camps. Near the end of their training in the States, they were drilled on how to work inside a prison and had classes on the law related to the treatment of prisoners under wartime conditions, including the relevant clauses of the Geneva Convention. The training they received on the handling and treatment of prisoners turned out to be critical because a scramble over the regular army battalion to which the 893rd would be assigned eventually led to the unit getting a mission to work inside rather than outside the wire—specifically, working the core holding area of a vastly overcrowded prison camp in Iraq.

Many specialists and junior NCOs realize that training can only go so far in preparing a soldier for his or her job on the ground. Simulations of running a prison camp made a difference, but even real-time training could not prepare the reservists for the cultural differences between the soldiers and the prisoners they handled or the working conditions of the prisons they took over. Megan Sutton's relatively meek demeanor is interestingly juxtaposed with both her junior NCO status and her strong family military lineage. While the pitch of her voice is high, the volume is muted as she explains anticipating that she and her fellow soldiers would be doing the impersonal work of guarding the perimeter of a prison and operating the towers where they would be watching the prison population from a distance. Megan, like many in the company, had hoped for such a mission, which would have clear operating guidelines and communication systems tied into the command structure when critical decisions needed to be made, including when to use weapons to stop escapes. Working inside the wire is "more intense and involved," and she found herself worrying constantly about how she would handle Iraqi prisoners whose language and customs she did not understand. Also, members of the company picked up information that the conditions at overseas prisons were far different than the simulated prisons at which the unit had trained while in the States. Overcrowding and the mixing of prisoners, youth with adults, common street criminals with highly valued prisoners of war, as well as maintaining a separate holding area for women, made many company members hope for a mission outside the wire.

Putting Boots on the Ground in Iraq

About a month and a half after the initial invasion of Iraq, the company was flown overseas to a staging camp in Kuwait. As the reservists prepared for their final destination near Baghdad, they faced another phase of uncertainty about what mission they would perform. As is always the case for reserve units, the company was to be assigned as a contingent to a regular army brigade. Enlistee and college student Troy Bixler, who has a love-hate relationship with the military, recalls with a certain level of contempt the 893rd's days in Kuwait, when the command structure fought about battalion and mission assignments:

> We didn't know what our mission was until three days before we started it. When we first got there, two battalions there, or whatever you want to call them, were fightin' over us, and one wanted us to patrol the streets of Baghdad while the other one wanted us to work the prison. Well, we weren't capable of patrolling the streets. We didn't have the equipment or the manpower. They were going to have us do it anyways. We were actually going to start the very next day, then they came down with the order that canceled that, that scrubbed that mission, and then we had to wait for our next one, which ended up being the prison.

The central command settled the dispute, assigning the company to work inside the wire of an already established enemy prisoner of war (EPW) camp, because another unit had already laid claim to working outside the wire. This internal prison mission was not what the soldiers had hoped for but was ultimately a safer mission than some of their sister MP companies received. Ben Matthews, who transferred to the 893rd following a simultaneous deployment in Iraq with a sister MP company, explains what life was like for reservists patrolling the streets on the mission for which the 893rd had originally been considered. Although there is genuine warmth to Ben's personality, smiles are hard to come by, and he keeps his somewhat vacant gaze focused on the concrete floor as he describes the difficulties his unit faced.

Our [training] was also EPW, but we were attached to the 4th Infantry
Division. So we had soldiers out kicking out doors, pulling people out.
It was really, you know, patrolling the streets, getting fired at. More
RPG [rocket propelled grenades], shot at, everything. The first month
we were there, I had more soldiers dodging death than I would have
liked to have. And our preparation was not for that mission. We had
insufficient weapons, insufficient equipment, a lot of other stuff that I
didn't feel comfortable myself sending troops out to do missions with.
We ended up using Iraqi weapons that we seized. They had some nice
weapons—I mean, we saw some pretty nice stuff. Brand new SAWs
[squad automatic weapon]—our equivalent to an M-60, which we don't
have anymore. . . . We seized about four or five of those. Ended up soldiers were making mounts and stuff for the top of the Humvees to
mount, it was a—it helped 'cause we didn't have the equipment to do it.

The reservists spoke of their disappointment in having been placed
inside the wire of the prison camp rather than in their specialty of exter-
nal work, but with few exceptions, they also frequently referenced a
sense of relief at having avoided missions like the one described by Ben
Matthews.

With the dispute over the nature of their mission settled, the company members approached the moment of moving into Baghdad, and
the soldiers realized how much they were going to rely on each other.
They quietly worried about their safety and wondered about who they
would be able to count on when they were in the war zone. The veterans of the stateside deployment worried about the recent transfers to
the company, younger soldiers worried if the older guys were up to the
task, and older, more experienced soldiers expressed concerns about
some of the young college students who had never been far from home
except for their months at Ft. McHenry. At the same time, unit members showed strong signs of being a company of soldiers that cared
about all of its members. Company bonding was evident as the unit
moved north toward Baghdad, with two of the platoons flying and one
convoying. Michelle Colton remembers the unit's final dinner together
as a company in Kuwait and the support other platoon members
offered to those assigned the dangerous job of convoying:

I think one of the scariest times was when we had the convoy from Kuwait to Baghdad, and my platoon was picked to convoy. The rest of the platoons flew from Kuwait, and I remember we were at the chow hall and one of the soldiers was just joking around and he said, "Okay, everybody. The people that are flying got to leave right now." And everybody drops their plates, and he says, "Just kidding." Ten minutes later that was real, and they had to leave, had to hurry up and pack all of their stuff, get ready to go in the C-130 to fly to Baghdad. And we were hugging each other good-bye, just in case that we didn't make it through the convoy, because they passed down [information] saying that no convoy has made it from Kuwait to Baghdad without suffering casualties. I'm like, "Okay, no problem."

And I remember none of us slept that night. I went outside the tent, and there's a floodlight. So I had some light, so I wrote the last letter, sealed it up, gave it to my first sergeant, and asked him to hold onto it just in case, 'cause he was flying. And he kept it and put it in his vest behind his plate.

And that night we woke up, and it was about 3:30 in the morning, and all of us was surrounding one Humvee, and all the light that we had was the headlights from the Humvees. And my sergeant said, "This is your convoy briefing." And he talks like what would happen if we get ambushed, if we get sniper attacks, if we get this, and the one thing that stood out was he is like, "If you get ambushed and blah, blah, blah, blah, blah, then these people will go back with a"— then he stopped, and he was like, "I'm not going to say it. I'm going to say wounded." Then we loaded up, and we drove. It was a two-day trip. It was hot. The kids, when they would come up to the Humvee, seeing them beg, but knowing how much you felt sorry for them, they could be the ones to hurt you. And then one of the greatest moments is that we arrived in Baghdad about an hour and a half late. So the rest of the company that's . . . in the building waiting for us are like on eggshells. "Where are they?" I remember when we were coming down the road, they see Humvees. We pull up and everybody's cheering and saying, "You guys made it!" I remember. . . . I took my helmet off, and all the females are like, "Colton!" I'm like, "Hey." It was a good feeling. You would think that we came home or something, but we just made it.

While those who convoyed north were dealing with the hazards common to convoys such as improvised explosive devices (IEDs) and roadside ambushes, the two platoons that flew to Baghdad were experiencing their own initiation into the reality of a war-zone deployment. With the sense of disbelief that sets in after contemplating the gravity of a dangerous situation, junior NCO Brad Whitman recalls that while flying into the Baghdad airport under the cover of darkness, the plane made an unannounced series of evasive maneuvers. All eyes were wide open in the darkness as the flight captain explained that they were "movin' and shakin' " to avoid an anti-aircraft missile launch.

Having made it safely to ground and transferred to the prison camp, they were greeted with the news that the prisoners were planning a riot that evening in hopes that the inexperience of the fresh military personnel on site would afford the prisoners an opportunity to escape. Even Lane Wright, a seasoned member of the 893rd with five years of prior active-duty experience and a civilian job as a prison guard, was unprepared for the reality of handling a prison uprising in a completely unfamiliar facility. The stress of the situation is conveyed through the tension in his voice as he explains,

> We had just got to Baghdad. We'd just got—we'd got to the airport. And they took us to this building where they said, "Okay, this is where you're going to be livin'. We can tell you that for sure, so start settlin' in." And we started cleaning the place up and lining up gear outside, and someone comes runnin' over and says, "You need to get over to the prison camp because they're going to riot tonight." And I said to the guy, I said, "I don't even know where the camp is." "Just go that way. Just go that way. You can't miss it."
>
> So we go over to the camp, and there's a big like empty warehouse-type building that all these soldiers are going into, and they hand out riot shields and batons and shin guards and flak vests all this stuff, and I started feeling sick to my stomach—just, "Oh my God, this is it. What did I get myself into?" After I pulled myself together a little—I mean, talk about when all the color leaves your face and you get that cold sweat and feel sick. But, you know, I'm collecting myself, and I thought, "Okay, I gotta check on [my two buddies] and make sure they're all right now that I got myself collected 'cause I'm sure they're

going through the same thing." So I'm checking my guys out, and this one—and it's not because she's a female—but this little mousy, a hundred-pound female just comes up to us and just chipper says, "So, it looks like we're going to get some spit time." And I said, *"Do you know where the fuck we are?!?"* And I will just never forget that. Never forget it.

When faced with the naïveté of his young, inexperienced female colleague, Lane is not only stunned by the reality of the fact that he must face a potential prisoner uprising but that he must do so with green reservists who seem to have no idea of the gravity of the situation. The tension in his story is broken by the incredulous anger he still feels toward her "chipper" demeanor in the face of what could have been serious danger. Fortunately, the riot rumors turned out to be false, and the members of the 893rd made it through a relatively peaceful night; however, the overcrowded, poorly constructed, and desperately under-manned prison camp was ripe for potential danger.

As time passed, company personnel established routines. Going inside the wire was always a tense experience, and the soldiers frequently did long shifts inside the prison. When not doing their jobs, they improved their living conditions, often jerry-rigging amenities, including a communication system for reaching family and friends back home. One deadly prison riot in particular interrupted their routines, as did assignments to convoy prisoners, which carried higher threats to safety and security. With time, the sense of company and reservist identity gave way to closer ties among smaller groups, platoons, work squads, and teams. The company appears less of a reference point than these smaller workgroups and buddy networks.[6]

Like the timing of their deployments and the nature of their missions, the point of exit from Iraq was also filled with uncertainty. The time spent on deployment in Ft. McHenry counted as part of what in these early years of the Iraq War was a two-year deployment clock for the Reserve, so nine months after arriving in Iraq, the company began preparations to return home. The soldiers felt proud that they had developed strong operating procedures at the prison camp. As they packed their equipment and planned to transfer the work of the prison camp to fresh soldiers, they still had to face the danger of traveling south to Kuwait. Most of the company would fly out of Baghdad Airport, a means of exit that had its own dangers, including getting to the airport along a highway that was often laced with roadside bombs. But even more dangerous was convoying back to Kuwait. Glenn Adams shows remarkable patience in his work and exhibits the calmness of someone who has grown accustomed to the military mantra of "hurry up and wait." His temperament serves him well as he calmly explains the daunting assignment of convoying vehicles and equipment out of Baghdad to Kuwait:

> The convoy got split in two because of the amount of vehicles we had, so [the company commander] volunteered to take the first group of vehicles and head down to Kuwait, and then an hour later I was supposed to move with the second group. And he made it through okay.
>
> I left, we had a problem with one of the trucks—not one of the unit's trucks, but a truck that was hauling our equipment had a problem with the brakes, and we had to get that fixed. So we ended up probably leaving almost two hours behind them. And then about sixty-five kilometers south of Baghdad, an IED went off right in front of our convoy. Yeah. There was actually two convoys. There was a convoy of—I believe they were engineers, and then we were directly behind them. But we were probably about three football field lengths, probably about three hundred meters from where it went off. So, I mean, we could have been in that area, but that's not the point of my story. That actually held us up for quite a while because they closed down the road. They totally shut it down until they could get an EOD [explosive ordinance disposal] team in there to see what was actually there and diffuse any remaining artillery shells that were buried in the road. So we ended up sitting there—we were stuck in traffic for almost nine hours. And finally we found an alternate route that took us over some rough terrain on a farmer's path, and we got to go around it. But it still ruined our chances of getting out of Iraq that day.

Going Home

The shared danger of exiting Iraq and the realization that the 893rd was headed home as an intact unit with no serious injury or loss of life seemed to reinvigorate the soldiers' broader identity as a company and as reservists who were veterans of the Iraq War. The welcome home ceremonies just before the December holiday period reinforced these common bonds even as the soldiers varied in their memories of these events. However, the soldiers quickly recognized that the bonds were likely to be transient because they were returning to their respective communities, jobs, and families rather than moving back to a home base that would enable and encourage their daily interactions with one another. Dennis Harris, whose close military buddies helped pull him through the emotional ups and downs of his on-again, off-again engagement, reflects on the passing qualities of the bonds that seem particular to reservist veterans:

> I was with these guys for—first through that year in Ft. McHenry and that year in Iraq. Coming back, you only see these guys once a month now. It's really hard to see these guys any other time because of whatnot, and they have other things to do. So you only see 'em once a month. And, like if I were to tell—someone joins the reserves and I were to tell them, I say, I'll tell 'em that's the hardest thing to do 'cause you only see these guys once a month now, and these guys are your friends and family and whatnot. So I guess that's really—you have fun, you have fun while you're on your deployments. You do, you get to know a lot of people, get to have a lot of friends and whatnot. But once you get off is when you start to miss 'em 'cause you only see 'em once a month, so I guess—and that's if they show up [for drill].

Relationships in the Company

For more than two years after 9/11, the 893rd remained a full-time functioning military unit. But as Dennis notes, the reservists of the company went in various directions after arriving home. After about a three-month break from drills, the company resumed its once-a-month, two-weeks-a-year drill schedule, but by the first weekend back at drill, the company was already reconstituted again. Now seasoned veterans, many of the soldiers returned to the 893rd's monthly routine, which included numerous promotions and restructuring of the teams, squads, and platoons. Other soldiers moved out of the military, having served out their contracts and chosen either to retire or to seek honorable discharges. Others transferred back to their original companies, and a few reservists simply stopped showing up for drill weekends. What remains are memories of their times together, of building identity and relationships with one another, along with the accompanying tensions that arise as boundaries are formed and reset over time. The architecture of their relationships with one another takes the shape of an hourglass with broad-based identity formation anchoring both the beginning and end of their deployments and more intense, small-group bonding the overriding feature as their experiences in the field mount, particularly when their boots are on the ground in Iraq.

Tensions between Reserve and Regular Army Components

The total force doctrine requires regular and reserve units to form close working relationships in the field. The 893rd and the regular army units to which it was assigned clearly developed a capacity to work in conjunction over time. However, at the rank-and-file level, the reservists report significant rifts between themselves and the regular army soldiers. These rifts, while a source of substantial tension, serve as a crucial source of bonding among the reservists as they forge their broad identity as a company of MPs with unique qualifications to do their jobs. Luis Balderas was an active-duty soldier before moving to the reserve to complete his original army contract, and he finds great irony in serving such extended deployments as a reservist rather than at any point during his four years of active-duty enlistment. Luis is typically good-natured during our conversation, but when he speaks, unprompted, of the treatment he and his colleagues of the 893rd received from active-duty personnel, he grows visibly angry. Capturing the sentiments of many in the 893rd whose sense of belonging in the company took shape as the reservists confronted hostility from the regulars after arriving at Ft. McHenry for their stateside deployment, Luis states,

> After all we endured down there at Ft. McHenry, and I don't want to say, I don't want to say abuse, but we got treated as literally redheaded stepchildren, the reservists versus the active duty. We outnumbered

them. We went like—we brought like 120 soldiers. And they only had like maybe 30 to secure their post. We . . . got treated like shit. . . . Why? We're reservists. 'Cause [they think] we don't know what we're doin'. We got more people in the reserves who know—who are cops, corrections, students studying all avenues of law enforcement, psychology, sociology, all that stuff that has a positive input for the whole operation, and they never, they never, they never seized the opportunity to say, "Hey, let's see what these guys are about." It was just more like us versus them.

The whole time. I mean, I made good friends there that were on the active-duty side, but overall, we got shitted on. And to me, that struck me very, very, very harsh because I would never think that the active-duty component would treat us like that—the reservists. Here we are, helpin' you out. I'm leaving all [my civilian job and family] behind to come down and help your ass. You live here. This is what you do here for a livin'. I did that for a livin', now I'm all done, and this is what I do for a livin'. Don't smack me in the face. Don't spit in my face. Tellin' me that, "Oh, you don't know what you're doing," or "This is the way we do it here." . . . I'm a soldier like you. I put a whole lot—I put my life on hold just to come help you guys out. . . . It was wrong. It was flat wrong, and everybody knew it.

Vince Stephenson is of similar NCO rank as Luis and has more than thirteen years of combined experience in the regular and reserve army. With his squared shoulders, stiff posture, buzz cut, and frequent use of terms such as "Yes, ma'am." and "No, ma'am," it would be difficult to miss his military training even if he was in civilian street clothes. Though he seems to be a military man through and through, Vince, like Luis, recognizes the unique qualities that reservists bring to their deployments as a consequence of civilian work experiences and is equally troubled by the regular army's failure to embrace the reservists as equals. He tries to explain why the regulars show such disrespect:

There is an animosity—I mean, basically, it's the whole "weekend warrior," and you have soldiers that are obviously active duty that are doing it every day of their life. For us in the reserves, in one sense, I get paid more money to deploy in the reserves than I do on active duty.

I'm a single soldier living in the barracks on active duty, I get deployed, I just make the same paycheck. When you're a single soldier in the reserves, you get your housing allowance, your food allowance. You start making more money. Active-duty soldiers being deployed doing the same thing, that automatically starts the animosity when they find out what we're making versus them. But then they don't realize that I have to pay for a home, a mortgage, everything else. So there, you get that animosity, plus, like I said, "weekend warriors."

Vince and several other members of the 893rd who have been in both the regular army and the reserves claim that a fundamental divide exists between these two components of the military because the regulars lack a robust civilian life experience. The reservists want respect for the civilian workplace qualifications and knowledge they bring to the field and an understanding that they too are making sacrifices in putting their civilian lives on hold. While a level of mutual understanding never appears to take shape, the fact that the reservists and regulars have to establish working routines tempers the hostilities that appear most acute in the early stages of field deployment.

Feeling they had proven their worth during their time at Ft. McHenry, it was again a slap in the face when the members of the 893rd redeployed overseas and found themselves back at the starting gate with the regulars with whom they were assigned to work closely. Again, the regulars refused to acknowledge the capabilities of the reservists after their initial deployment to Iraq and denied access to services, including telecommunications systems that enable the regulars to keep in contact with friends and family members back in the States. The hostile treatment by regulars enabled the company members once again to reestablish common bonds as they drew on their civilian skills to jerry-rig Internet access to home and found ways to make their lives more comfortable in an inhospitable environment. The rift and the corresponding closing of ranks among the reservists in response to the initial hostility and testing by the regulars came at a crucial time because the company had substantially changed its composition between deployments, and many of the reservists were just getting to know one another, this time amid much greater danger.

Divisions within the Company

The strong sense of company identity that takes shape in the early phase of deployments does not come without the typical divisions evident in most work environments. Rank matters within the company and is backed by a stringent disciplinary system that exceeds those operating in most work environments, including those associated with civilian law enforcement and corrections. Complicating the acceptance of authority in the company is the fact that one's civilian status may not comport with one's authority in the 893rd. Many of the company's noncommissioned and commissioned officers come from the lower ranks in the public and private sector, and a few are unemployed or in and out of the civilian workforce because they lack the skills and education necessary to secure stable jobs in a shifting economy. Expanding on the frustrating parts of his love-hate relationship with the army, Troy Bixler resents the authority that some lower-status civilians have over him in the military. He reveals the below-surface rankling that is a product of the company's authoritarian structure.

> [We] had guys who over there, you know, they're E6s—which was a squad leader position—you're pretty high rank in soldier at that point, but back in the civilian life they'd work at like, you know, Wal-Mart full-time, and they still live with their mom. And yet over there, they can tell me what to do and dole out punishment. They can actually punish you, be it extra duty, [make you] write up, like, a report and everything else. Who are they to do that except for the fact that they're your superior officer? So in that respect, at times I was very angry because I felt that there were times that I was really mistreated by the chain of command. What are you gonna do?

Like civilian law enforcement and corrections organizations, degrees of military experience matter, and, as is evident in Lane Wright's story of the potential prison riot, this becomes particularly acute as a source of differencing and tension when the members of the unit recognize that their safety depends on the actions of those around them. A tension point within the 893rd revolves around those who enter the reserves after a stint in the regular army, in contrast to those who have experience only as reservists. NCOs are more likely to have regular army experience, and many of them have been deployed prior to 9/11 in dangerous operations ranging from Panama to Bosnia. These senior soldiers voice strong concerns about the least experienced among those they command, particularly focusing on the uncertainty about how they will respond to wartime conditions.

Keith Jackson is among the most somber of the company members, and this weightiness is reflected in both the tone and tempo of his methodical speech pattern. The rigid carriage of his tall frame punctuates his seriousness. As a junior NCO with ten years of professional military experience prior to transferring to the Army Reserve, Keith has a great appreciation for the magnitude of wartime deployments and little patience for the naïveté that comes with green soldiers. He remembers that when they arrived at the prison camp, the most inexperienced recruits were excited about the possibility of seeing action. They were, as he says, all "lock and load" and "gung-ho." As the platoon starts to set up living quarters in a warehouse of the prison camp, a U.S. ordnance team begins detonating explosives nearby. Jolted by the explosions and unaware of their origin, Keith and two other NCOs grab their weapons and head outside to investigate what they assumed was an enemy attack. As he recalls looking back at the less experienced soldiers, he recounts grimly,

> All they did was just sat up in their beds. They just sat straight up, and everybody looked towards me. . . . By the time I left and came back and my sergeant's coming, they were sitting straight up in bed. *Nobody moved.*

Jackson calls that a defining moment, the point he realized that despite their talk and training, many of the enlistees were ill prepared for the conditions of war.

> Nobody grabbed a weapon other than those other two people. That stands out a lot. And that's when I tell people, "We weren't ready, okay." And as ready as you think you are, you're not ready. And when soldiers were sayin', "Lock and load," and all gung-ho, ready to do

some damage to some—the enemy, per se, it would upset me especially being in law enforcement. It's like, "You're not ready. Something just happening, you didn't even react. So stop acting like you're
ready to shoot somebody, 'cause you've never shot anybody. You've
never seen anybody shot, and you've never been shot at. So you don't
know what your reaction's going to be. So let's just calm down and be
ready just to do the job as it comes along."

Bands of Brothers . . . and Sisters

As their deployment to Iraq grips them, the members of the 893rd reveal
a shift in their interactions with one another. The salience of the company and their broad identity as reservists, as distinct from regular
army, gives way to more particularized bonding. While racial identity
was not a basis for forming close bonds within the company, the
females in the 893rd developed close-knit groups soon after arriving in
Iraq. Unrevealed in their narratives is whether their tightening of bonds
resulted more from their struggles to secure a degree of privacy amid
very difficult living conditions at the prison camp or to their feeling less
safe among a sea of men disconnected from their home lives. Whatever
their reasons, the women stick together and watch each other's backs
more closely in Iraq.[7] Michelle Colton makes clear the salience of the
women's bonding with one another and their distancing from the men
while garrisoned at the makeshift prison for nearly a year.

> There was only four females in my entire platoon, and the three or
> four of us became very close, and believe it or not, we took care of
> what we needed to take care of. We didn't have to depend on the guys
> or anything like that because the guys were with the guys. Basically,
> we took care of each other, so that's the friendship that I built with
> them.

Michelle also reveals what is evident in the narratives of women and
men alike talking about their Iraq deployment. The reference to the
company and their being reservists as distinct from regulars gives way
to the centrality of their membership in the platoon, the subunit that is

essential to their daily work routines and living quarters. Each platoon establishes its own turf and relational dynamics, and with a sense of frustration, junior NCO Ian Farber depicts platoon turf in the way that urban gang members invoke the rules of association related to their 'hoods.

> We have three platoons, and it's more or less, okay, here's first platoon—that's their people. Here's second. And it's us and them. I mean its just totally separated from each other 'cause you can't walk into their house without somebody sayin', "Hey, this is second platoon's house. What are you doin' over here?" And nobody from second platoon's going to walk in third platoon's house without getting jumped or beat up, you know. That's how we subvert ourselves, you know. . . . But no, if you put us all together, we work as a unit, okay. But at the same time, our units are still separated down. I mean, we can work all together, but there's always going to be that—not friction, but that gray area of first, second, and third.

The closeness the soldiers felt toward the others in their platoons came at an expense to their relationships with members of the other platoons. The specialists reference members of other platoons in derogatory ways as they invoke a language of bonding with one another. They also claim that their platoon NCOs, their sergeants, reinforced the boundaries of the platoons and that this process carried forward to their squad leaders, the even smaller work groups that define everyday life in the 893rd. Junior NCO Garrett Wesner depicts the strong divide between the platoons:

> We had our close people, like when everyone in the first platoon was pretty close, but everyone in the first platoon for the most part didn't like anyone in the second platoon, and anyone in the second platoon didn't like anyone in the first platoon, and we both didn't like people in the third platoon.

Garrett goes on to say that the platoon leaders had some motivation to build an allegiance that would make the job easy for them.

At the scale of the squad and the teams within the platoons, the popularized notion of a band of brothers takes shape within the 893rd. These are the small work groups within a platoon that perform the same tasks during the same shifts of duty. Some of the squads and teams are made up of reservists who trained together stateside and come from the same places, either diverse urban communities or white rural communities. Many of the reservists romanticize their squads and the cliques they formed within them, almost parroting the scripts of popular movies about soldiering in wartime. Others provide a more personalized rendition of their bonds that can permeate teams and squad organizational structure but rarely cross platoon lines. Brad Whitman, who involuntarily transferred into the 893rd along with several reservists from a former company, at first has a difficult time putting into words the importance of his ties to his military colleagues but ends up talking eloquently of the ways in which the line between friend and family becomes blurred:

> The places I've gone, the things that I've went through, I couldn't have gotten through them without other people, without other soldiers, and I don't look at them as just best friends or fellow soldiers. Some of them I look at as family. I mean, it's to the point where you know that person so well that you wake up, you go to guard mount, and you're looking at them and know that something's wrong. You can sense it. It's something with my wife—it's the same thing. And I look at that as somebody being family. That you definitely, you think about it at night, would you give your life for this fellow soldier or to the point where, to the extent where I would say, yes, I would, because they are family to me. . . . These soldiers become your brother, your sister, your dad. They become people who you now have to go to ask, "Can you help me out? Hey, there's something wrong with my vest, can you fix it for me?" Something like that. So or on a more meaningful note, those are the people who you go to and say, "Hey, listen, I'm having trouble. I just can't sleep at night. I can't deal with this. I need to talk." So, or those are the people who, it's one of those things where I have a saying and it says, a friend is one who, something about a friend is one who makes you laugh or listens to you or something, but

a true friend is one who helps you carry the bodies. And when you go through things like that, when you see that, it's tough. It's tough for you, it's tough for them, but you deal and you cope with it *together*.

For Brad and others, these bonds trump those of his civilian life, and he now calls on the people from his unit to help him traverse problems that arise back home. However, others were far less comfortable with these tight groups and saw them as undermining esprit de corps. Pat Bickford, a junior NCO who relished his deployment job in the 893rd far more than his civilian job as a customer service representative for a large chain store, is very clear about how much tension and infighting the cliques or bands of brotherhood produced while the company was in Iraq:

> Some of the cliques were bad, and what I mean by that is some of these guys just made fun of other people constantly, and I'm not exaggerating. When you sit there for eight hours picking fun of a particular female, there's issues—I mean, that's not showing any support of fellow soldiers, and it especially is not what that person needs either, and she heard it. It got back to her. That's for an example, but—some situations, yeah, I saw some people stick together, but at other times I saw just backstabbing and so much gossip and everything over there. I just wanted to shake my head. I just had to draw myself away from all that crap. It made me mad. . . . I would have to say that the commander should have said something like about all the negative speaking out that was going on, especially within our platoon. Put his foot down and say, "Now, enough with the negative comments because negative atmosphere doesn't help anything with morale, and [if] you haven't got anything good to say, don't say it at all." I mean, seriously speaking, it doesn't help at all. I heard a lot of negative things over there about the unit, about individual soldiers, and it does honestly bring morale down.

Pat saw these cliques and bands of reservists as undermining morale and regarded much of the male bonding as achieved at the expense of individual soldiers, particularly females. These affronts to women, perpetrated by close-knit groups of men, may explain why the women in the company formed their own band of sisters.

War Veterans with Civilian Lives

Whether their memories of particular cliques and bands of fellow reservists are positive or negative, the immediate reintroduction of reservists to family members and civilian workmates after returning home jolts them into confronting their sense of identity all over again. Throughout most of our conversation, junior NCO Barry Watts has the playfulness of a class clown and takes pleasure in occasionally trying to anticipate our questions, but his demeanor and tone shift dramatically when asked to describe his transition out of active duty. Without hesitation, he dryly states,

> Quick and swift, like death itself. It was pretty fast. It was so fast I still felt like I was on active duty. I don't think like the soldiers had enough time to sit down. We had one session with the chaplain. The chaplain would debrief and talk about stuff, fears when we get back home. I don't think that was enough. I think that was a step in the right direction. I think we should have more time to just sit and talk amongst each other, because like when I go through stuff at home and I have problems, I feel better talking with guys I've been through it with, and I'm more comfortable to relate, you know. It's like when they have problems, they call me, or I'll call them. I don't think we had enough time to just sit, you know, in group sessions and just talk about some of our fears, just kind of console each other. We were going back and forth, I was feeling a little love generating in the room, but it was like only a one-day thing. It wasn't like continued process, like, okay, this week we're going to do this, all right, and next week we will have the same session, then next week, you know. 'Cause you need somebody to talk to.

All of these citizen-soldiers realize that the close bonds will give way to more transient relationships as they recycle to their weekend drills and occasional sharing of beers afterward. The suddenness of their transition from soldiers on a war front to civilians with friends, family members, and coworkers shifts the scale of their military identities back to the broad from the particular. They are veterans of war and reservists who all came back alive from Iraq. They identify closely with other veterans and other reservists who have been to Iraq and Afghanistan.

As they go through the complex process of readapting to their civilian lives, they realize that their unique experience of being deployed, particularly in a war zone, represents a crack between them and the civilian friends, family members, and coworkers with whom their lives again become entangled. Glenn Adams expresses more disappointment than anger as he reflects the feelings of many in the 893rd about the unease they feel after their initial return to the States and what they suspect most civilians are thinking.

> It was odd, and actually both times I came back, it was odd. I mean, people welcoming you home and are glad you're home and want to know what it was all about, but both times it's like the interest anybody shows on a lot of different levels is over very quick. And I don't think a lot of people are prepared for that. Now, when we came back from Iraq, [the army] actually warned us of that before we came back: "People"—and they were pretty blunt—"people really don't care where you've been or what you've done." I mean, "Yes, they'll welcome you back, but what they're thinking is, 'Hey, you've been gone. Someone else has been doing your job. It's time for you to put that behind you and get back to what you're supposed to be doing.'" And there was more of that this time than [after the return from Ft. McHenry].

The returning reservists receive debriefings warning them that citizens will welcome them home but not embrace the memories of their shared experiences as soldiers. This runs true to Glenn's experience and that of many other members of the 893rd as civilians expect these reservists to get on with the civilian responsibilities friends, family, and coworkers have covered for so long.

Left with a Stigma

As the members of the company work to bring their civilian identities and responsibilities into alignment, they are dogged by the divide between being reservists and regular army. They are proud of their reservist status, but many citizens presume that being a reservist means that a soldier was on the sidelines of the war effort. Randy Stires is an enlistee barely into his twenties who was deployed both in the States and in Iraq. With the boyish innocence of a child who unexpectedly receives adult praise, Randy tells a story about going back to work as an exterminator and having his boss proudly introduce him to a couple of guys who have joined the pest control business while he was in Iraq:

> And I remember my boss introduced me to several of the other guys that were new when I went to work, and when he said, "Oh yeah, he just got out of the army. He just got back from overseas," they were like, "So, you were a year in Kuwait, right? You were a reservist in Kuwait, right?" "No, I was in Baghdad." "You were in Baghdad?" I was like, "Yes, I was in Baghdad. . . . You want me to prove it to you? I can prove it to you."

Randy resents the fact that he has to defend his status as a veteran reservist deployed to the war zone. When he goes out for beers later in the week with the new employees, who were formerly regular army, he learns that only one of them had been deployed overseas—to Germany. Ironically, Randy is stuck defending the reservists as these former active-duty soldiers "try and lump reservists as a lazy group." Having spent two years proving that he is more than the pejorative "weekend warrior," Randy is aggravated by this interaction.

Just as the members of the 893rd were settling into their civilian lives while holding onto their identities as reservist veterans of war, the Abu Ghraib scandal broke in the news. Members of the 893rd vividly recall these moments as well as the decisions they had to make about how to describe their jobs while deployed in Iraq. Some decided to pull back from any conversations about Abu Ghraib, while others wanted civilians to know that the 893rd competently handled a very tough job policing an overcrowded, ill-equipped prison camp—*not* Abu Ghraib. Glenn Adams shows no hesitation to confront the issue and defends the company's job while deployed in Iraq:

> I have no problem telling them what mission we did. Some people totally avoid that whole thing. But I'll tell them I guarded Iraqi pris-

oners over there. And of course right away they would ask, "Well, were you at that prison, or did similar things happen at your prison?" So it's affected us all, and I—the bigger thing that has affected us all is just the way the news stories again are not totally accurate, and we know that 'cause we were over there. But especially the initial ones pretty much labeled all the reserves as being this undertrained group of rogue warriors that are over there doing their own thing and have no clue what they're doing and had no direction and just doing whatever. And that's not the way we operated. I mean, we went over there, we were under the same brigade as that prison, and we weren't getting direction from them either. We set up our own SOPs [standard operating procedures], . . . and I think we did a pretty darn good job of it, so. And anyone in our unit would say that.

The reservists of the 893rd left for their initial deployment stateside and soon found themselves defending their competency in front of the regular army. They had to confront the stigma associated with being "weekend warriors" both at Ft. McHenry in the States and when they assumed responsibilities inside the wire of the enemy prisoner of war camp. Returning after nearly two years of back-to-back deployments, they experience the stigma once again, this time as MP reservists whose job closely paralleled the assignment of the reservists whose work at Abu Ghraib has given the entire reserve system a black eye. For most of the reservists, returning to civilian life demands so much of them that they do not to dwell on the stigma they experienced as the first broad public questioning of the Iraq War emerged from the images of Abu Ghraib. This is one more circumstance among the many changes in their lives since 9/11.

three

Joining the Reserve

"It's a Great Place to Start"

I was looking at the Web site, and . . . they showed a garrison MP waving traffic through, standing at the gates saluting people, and I was like, "I can do that. I can do that. No problem." So I joined up, thinking that's exactly what I was going to do. . . . Then off to basic training and AIT [advanced individual training]. Our drill sergeants were yelling about going to war and all stuff like that, and I like didn't do it out in the open, but I secretly was like, "Yeah, right. I'm not gonna go to war. By the time I get out of here, first off, this entire thing [the war in Iraq] is gonna be over, and then I'm a reservist, so I'm probably gonna wind up being stuck in an airport, or directing traffic on a base, that's probably as far as it's gonna go." Yeah. Talk about having my little dream shattered.

—Enlisted Army Reservist Peter Corell

Peter Corell never wanted to be a full-time soldier. He describes himself as an average guy who likes "normal stuff"—camping, going to nightclubs, and shopping at the mall. He works out at the gym every day with his friends, and while he is not a large man, his physical training pays off. His best friend, who joined the regular army following high school, urged Peter to join the military on several occasions, but Peter countered that he did not see himself wearing the uniform or being on the receiving end of a continual flow of orders. The possibility that MP reserve service might at some point look identical to active-duty service never entered Peter's mind. For him, joining the Reserve meant that he could make a part-time commitment to the military to get a leg up in the competitive applicant pool for the Federal Bureau of Investigation (FBI). Taking advantage of the training in military police garrison work, Peter thought, would surely mimic the skills necessary in civilian law enforcement.

The idea of utilizing the Army Reserve as an avenue for pursuing civilian goals is not something that Peter made up on his own. He was simply following the Army Reserve's marketing campaign:

> Army Reserve. Your Life. With more meaning. The Army Reserve gives you the freedom to pursue your goals—and the skills and discipline to make them a reality. As a civilian and a soldier, you'll continue your career or education while training close to home and standing ready to serve your country.[1]

Army Reserve recruitment campaigns, even those after 9/11, feature the notion that being a citizen-soldier is a part-time commitment that can be worked in and around an individual's civilian priorities, duties, goals, and obligations.[2] The advertising campaigns sell to new recruits the idea that their civilian and soldier statuses are complimentary, with the soldier status serving as an avenue for achieving civilian desires. In fact, they are not coequal statuses. Civilian and soldier are competitive positions embedded within an uneven institutional playing field on which, with few exceptions, soldier is the trump card over every other civilian position. Prior to 9/11, reserve service was primarily an issue of citizen-soldiering. For thousands of reservists, including the members of the 893rd, that ended when the Twin Towers came crashing down.

Pathways to Reserve Enlistment—Instrumental and Cultural Orientations

In 1971, when the Senate Armed Services Committee was debating the possibility of ending conscription, Senator Edward Kennedy warned

that moving to an all-volunteer army of professionals and citizen-soldiers would result in "poor people fighting rich men's wars."[3] More
than thirty years later, we find that many members of the 893rd came to
the military to address individual economic conditions. Citizens who
enlist for these *instrumental orientations* use the Reserve to achieve economic stability and enhance social mobility. Some members of the
893rd wanted resources so that they could go to college, knowing that
their families could not afford the mountain of bills. Others were positioning themselves for the expansion of corrections or law enforcement
jobs, believing that military experience, particularly as MPs, would give
them an edge in competing for positions in the civilian criminal justice
system. Still others looked specifically to the paycheck they would
receive in the reserves to help them out of immediate financial troubles.
And some looked beyond immediate financial needs and saw reserve
service as a way to generate retirement savings.

The relationship between economic conditions and military reserve
recruiting is supported by a recent study commissioned by the Office of
the Secretary of Defense that provides strong evidence that poor economic conditions prompt "voluntary" reserve enlistments. Using state-
level aggregate data, the RAND Corporation study shows that economic, demographic, and policy factors such as high unemployment
rates, higher average college tuition rates, and increased educational
incentives offered for National Guard and Reserve increase enlistments
in the reserves component of the military.[4] Simply put, a tightening
American economy that squeezes lower- and middle-class families' abilities to provide for themselves and their children increases participation
rates in the Army Reserve and National Guard.

While recruitment studies capture the underlying conditions that
trigger citizens to be instrumental in their decisions to join the Reserve,
the focus on economic trends and enlistment patterns neglects the
significance of *cultural orientations,* where citizens see joining the
Reserve as a way to enhance their sense of themselves.[5] Cultural orientations emerge over time, first taking hold at a young age and continuing as a logical path to adulthood in a culture that offers few rites of
passage. This orientation is revealed through references to hobbies such

as building a personal collection of military memorabilia, childhood play that focuses on simulations of war, and continuous exposure to heroic images of war offered by America's entertainment industry. It is also revealed in conversational reflections when reservists express their pride in continuing a long family legacy of military service.

The complexity of enlistment decisions—decisions that can be as quick as the spur-of-the-moment or ten years in the making—take place within a web of interpersonal relationships, personal identities, and institutional forces and draw on both instrumental and cultural orientations. The decision to enlist, whether initially in the active or reserve component, can be thought of as loosely falling along a spectrum with end points ranging from a purely cultural orientation to that of a purely economic orientation; however, few reservists reveal exclusively instrumental or cultural orientations that place them on the extreme ends of the spectrum. Instead, they invoke some combination of both cultural and instrumental factors that fall into five general points along this continuum.[6] We define these five pathways as follows:

> *Destiny Fulfilled*—most closely aligned with a cultural orientation, with reservists invoking military service as part of their self-imagination; frequently coupled with references to long family legacies of military service.
>
> *Making a Mark*—a cultural orientation in which the decision to join the reserves is a rite of passage to adulthood—usually manhood—and typically in direct opposition to other family members' dreams for the individual.
>
> *One for the Recruiter*—for these reservists, the person most credited with influencing the decision to join the reserves is a military recruiter who appealed to a combination of cultural and instrumental orientations.
>
> *A Way Out*—an instrumental orientation with citizens joining the full-time active component of the military to escape confining economic or family conditions.
>
> *A Way Up*—an instrumental orientation with the military as a primary source of social mobility through benefits such as educational reimbursements for college expenses.

Destiny Fulfilled and a Dream Comes True

For many members of the 893rd, joining the military is something they always wanted to do, having engaged since childhood in behaviors that anticipate becoming a soldier. They reminisce about playing war with other kids during Boy Scout meetings or spending time with their GI Joe action figure collections. Jorge Mercado, who had joined the Reserve twelve years earlier despite serious objections from his parents, glances down at his watch and smiles as he recalls,

> When I was younger, I just—I was always into military stuff. Weapons. My watch has been on twenty-four-hour time since high school, since my sophomore year or something. . . . I'm still a patriot at heart, and I was always a patriot. I was a patriot when being a patriot wasn't cool.

These reservists invoke cinematic warrior imagery as they talk about their reasons for joining the regular army or Reserve. They draw on the narratives of films such as *Death before Dishonor*, in which Marine Gunnery Sergeant Burns, a virtual one-man army, rejects the military rule book and crippling bureaucratic red tape to save his brothers in arms. Likewise, Sylvester Stallone portrayed John Rambo, a disenfranchised Vietnam War Special Forces veteran who single-handedly rescues long-forgotten prisoners of war in the 1985 film *Rambo: First Blood, Part II*. In addition to referencing celluloid military heroes, these reservists also draw on actual images of successful military campaigns. Junior NCO Todd Kirkendall was affected during his adolescence not by Hollywood's fictional imagery but by watching the real events of the first Gulf War unfold during the early 1990s.

> I guess I'd trace it back to sitting at home and watching the first Gulf War occur on television. I saved a newspaper from every day from the day the war started until the cease-fire, and for some reason, I was just engulfed by it. . . . I was twelve or thirteen, somewhere around that.

This early identification with military culture did not develop within a vacuum. With only one exception, these men and women grew up in families with long legacies of military service, and they express a strong obligation to continue this line of national service. Todd's father was a military police officer with service in Germany, his uncle was in Vietnam, and his grandfather had been in Korea. Todd may have wanted to be in the military since his fascination with the first Gulf War and may have wanted to continue the family legacy, but he chose reserve service as a tentative entry point "because I figured if I didn't like it, it was only one weekend a month. But if I did love it, I could just switch over and go active." The tension of wanting to join the military to fulfill a family legacy but not wanting to commit one's life to full-time service is echoed by a young enlisted soldier, Dan Mulcahy.

❖ Dan Mulcahy

There is a bluntness about Dan Mulcahy that comes in part from having grown up in a working-class family and from just having served two years under military deployments where salty language is the norm. While Dan projects a sense of relaxed self-confidence, the fact that he carries at least four pocket knives makes us wonder what he is protecting himself from. With three years of service under his belt, Dan epitomizes this pathway to citizen-soldiering. Exposed to military culture through a variety of avenues in his childhood, Dan grew up with the expectation that he would follow in his family's tradition. He enlisted in the Reserve between his junior and senior years of high school and explains matter-of-factly the various influences on his decision:

> I was told since I was real little that if you're a Mulcahy, you join the military. You serve somehow, someway. Since everybody jokes around and calls me "Lieutenant Dan" [from the 1994 film *Forrest Gump*]; because since World War I on, I had a family member or two in at least every war almost. There's only been one that hasn't served in some type of combat, and that was my dad, and my uncle because he refused to join. But everybody else has. . . . My dad always had me watch war movies, which now they're always saying it ain't a good thing for kids to watch. That's all I watch anymore. All kinds of action flicks. I always wanted to be Rambo myself, but it never really happened.

Dan Mulcahy actually looks quite a bit like a shorter, slightly darker-haired version of Lieutenant Dan, played in the film by Gary Sinise. Lieutenant Dan was Forrest Gump's Vietnam platoon leader, who was devastated by the fact that he did not die on the battlefield as had a member of his family in every American war since the revolution. While Dan Mulcahy jokes about the comparison, he takes great pride in knowing that the members of his family returned alive from their various wars.

Dan Mulcahy's family members fully expected him to join the active component of a military branch of his choice, and they were quite surprised when Dan made a part-time rather than full-time commitment by enlisting in the reserves. His hesitations regarding military life are revealed in his body language, as he shifts around uncomfortably in his BDUs and jokes with us about our civilian attire, saying that he would much rather be wearing black-colored civilian garb than the browns and dark greens of his camouflage, which do not really suit him. By joining the reserves, Dan thought he would be meeting the competing demands in his life—the family that expected military service, the girlfriend who did not want him involved in the military, and his desire to go to college and join the law enforcement community (ultimately the FBI). Caught off guard by the events of 9/11, Dan's plan did not work out as well as he had intended. Since the terrorist attacks occurred during his senior year of high school, he became a full-time soldier following his high school graduation. Instead of weaving his military service into the fabric of his civilian life, he had to stitch little strands of his civilian life into the fabric of his military life. While Dan's family is proud of his tour of duty in Iraq, college has never happened, and his girlfriend broke up with him while the company was mobilizing for Iraq.

Making a Mark

For some of the soldiers traveling along this second pathway, joining the military tends to be a direct act of defiance of their parents' wishes. Vince Stephenson recalls wanting to enlist during high school despite his father's and brother's objections. As someone who looks like he could have been the model for the GI Joe action figure, it is difficult to imagine Vince not serving in the military, and with a resolute tone he states, "Once I turned eighteen, I was able to sign and didn't need my parents' permission. So I go, went ahead, and did it around them, their wishes." Other soldiers relay similar stories of being drawn to military culture that reveal a rite of passage to adulthood and fulfill the need to achieve a personal goal or growth experience. A number of these young men found turning eighteen and making a decision without parental approval to be important, and all of the soldiers within this pathway are men. They are living out the ideology of the recruiting campaigns— "Your life. With more meaning." These individuals join the military reserves as a way to distinguish themselves as men among men. Other military slogans came into play for these men as well. Lane Wright, who began his military service in the active component, recounts a previous popular military recruiting campaign, "They used to say in a commercial, 'It's a great place to start,' and I think that's perfect." For the majority of these men who joined the reserve system directly rather than first serving on active duty, as Lane had, the Reserve is a way to make a mark but avoid a twenty-four/seven commitment to the military—or so they thought.

Travis Shaffer, who grew up in a pacifist family, chuckles when he recalls thinking of joining the reserves when he was seventeen. Travis thought he would get a taste of the military culture that had been denied him throughout his entire childhood: "Just that I could experience the military, and then I thought I could do a little bit, and this is one way to get in without making a real commitment—well, everyday commitment, I thought." Among the soldiers trying to make a mark, Ian Farber is perhaps most explicit about his desire to find a way to distinguish himself among family members.

❖ Ian Farber

As we begin our conversation in a quiet conference room on a drill weekend afternoon, Ian Farber displays a sense of eagerness for someone, somewhere, to hear his story. Ian now believes that being a reservist is the toughest job a person can undertake. Embroiled in the midst of a bad divorce involving a "Dear John" phone call just before departing from Iraq and trying to raise his teenage daughter as a single parent, Ian firmly believes that "for the last two years, my life was taken away from me because I got deployed to Ft. McHenry and then I got deployed overseas to Iraq." Ian has come to realize the high price of his initial decision sixteen years earlier to join the reserves. Thinking back to his rationale for joining, Ian explains,

> Actually I'm the very first one of [several] generations to ever join the military. I thought it would be, back then, it would be the coolest thing because I was the only one. Go back generation after generation, it's like I just couldn't find nobody. It's like, "Man, who was in the military in my family?" But after the search, it was, like, nobody. So I thought, "You know, I'm going to be the first one," and I am still the first one to this day 'cause all my cousins, they're like, "I can't do that. I can't do this." So it's not like I'm one up on [them] or anything, it's just that I did it. You know I did it for myself, more or less.

Indeed, making his decision to join caused quite a stir with his parents.

> As soon as my senior year was done in June, I left in August. . . . My mom and dad were flippin' out. 'Cause at that time I was seventeen going on eighteen, and they're like, "No you can't join, you can't join, blah, blah, blah." I'm like, "I'm doin' this for me, you know. I want to do it for myself. . . . I want to show my family, I'm going to show my brother that I can become what I am today."

As Ian proudly relays this story of his initial enlistment in the Reserve, the sentiments he expresses echo the army's campaign slogan, "Be all you can be." While those seeking to make a mark received little or no encouragement from their families, unlike the soldiers along the destiny pathway, members of this cohort are driven to enlistment by many of the same cultural forces. Voluntarily joining the reserves in direct defiance of parental wishes serves as a benchmark for personal achievement and a passage to adulthood.

One for the Recruiter

With the wars in Iraq and Afghanistan continuing long after 9/11, documentary films critical of the use of military force made their way to distribution. Michael Moore's 2004 *Fahrenheit 9/11* and Eugene Jarecki's 2006 *Why We Fight* offer vivid accounts of military recruiters targeting young men and women of limited economic means, hoping to persuade them to enlist in the armed services. Moore's film follows U.S. Marine recruiters targeting young, economically disadvantaged black men at an urban shopping center. Jarecki's film in part follows the recruitment process of a young, economically disadvantaged white male as he tries to cope with the loss of his mother and his inability to develop a clear plan for himself. Like a helpful big brother, the army recruiter featured in *Why We Fight* shows the young man that if he just signs on the dotted line, the military will take care of his problems.

In our conversations with members of the 893rd, we heard similar stories of persistent recruiters and their efforts to enlist young men and women. These determined efforts are effective in identifying the benefits of the reserves, focusing primarily on the instrumental benefits of part-time military service as a way to achieve civilian goals. Whether recruited straight out of high school or on college campuses, these young reservists talk of having been targeted for repeat visits by persistent recruiters. Darnell Powell recalls the recruiting efforts that took place at his state college: "Well, it was '96, my sophomore year—no, freshman year in college, and the recruiters kept bugging me and bugging me and telling me what type of office I could get." The possibility of enlisting in the military was not foreign to these men and women prior to their contact with recruiters, but these soldiers credit their decision to join the Reserve to a particular recruiter who convinced them that the military would make their civilian goals achievable.

❖ Vanessa Hendricks

As a self-described "military brat," Vanessa Hendricks grew up with the constant cultural reminder of military service. With her long hair pulled back in a tight bun, her perfectly stiff posture, and fingers that are continuously curled in half fists in accordance with military preference, Vanessa certainly embodies the internalization of military rules and regulations. Although her deep voice has a coarseness that could serve her well should she decide to make the military her career, Vanessa's real passion is working with young children, and she looks forward to being an elementary school teacher. In spite of having grown up in the shadow of the military, Vanessa is quick to point out that her father never pressured her to join. This, however, did not stop the military recruiting office from doing so while Vanessa was away at college.

> Well, my father is military. He was military intelligence, so I've grown up most of my life seeing him in uniform and the whole military life, living on a base and everything, so, that kinda pushed me towards that field. But I knew I didn't want it 'cause I love kids, so I wanna be a teacher, so I knew I didn't want to do it full time. So I decided if I do Reserve, they'll pay for my school or a portion of my school, and it can just benefit my family because they won't have to be dishing out all the money. . . . The recruiter had been bangin' down my door since I was a junior in high school, and I didn't think I was ready, 'cause you leave over the summer, and you want to spend the time with your friends and whatnot. But by the time I became a sophomore in college, I started thinking it's not going to be that bad, so plus I figured its going to be challenging, and I like challenging stuff.

Challenging experiences are exactly what Vanessa got: the timing of her enlistment was such that her first and so far only deployment has been to Iraq. She wants to continue her civilian pursuit of a teaching certification far more than to be redeployed. Thinking about her future as a teacher, Vanessa raps on the conference room table and states, "Knock on wood, as long as we don't get another call."

Under the continual prodding of the military recruiter's office, Vanessa ultimately signed up with the reserves with the idea that both instrumental and cultural needs would be met. On the instrumental front, joining the reserves would be a way to alleviate her parents having to foot her college education. Culturally, the military service would enable her to live up to a personal challenge. In this way, the recruiters hooked Vanessa with the promise echoed in the recruiting campaigns—

having a part-time job that would provide new challenges while giving a young person the skills and money to become an independent adult.

A Way Out

One of the instrumental pathways involves those soldiers who join active-duty full-time service as an avenue to escape the travails of civilian life. These men, all of whom were now in their thirties and forties, eventually transferred from active duty to reserve status and together represent the most experienced group of soldiers within the company, with a combined eighty years of reserve and active-duty service. Looking back on his decision to enlist more than twenty years earlier, Derek Henry laughs nostalgically as he talks about his "voluntary" enlistment as a way to avoid incarceration.

> I used to always get in trouble a lot, to be honest, and I was actually given a choice with one of the state police officers, but really one of the commanders 'cause he knew my family, and it was like, "We could like prosecute and go to jail or do some good and go to military 'cause you are from a decent family." I guess I was the bad egg. And I actually chose to go to the military.

Derek is a solidly built man who looks like he could still handle himself in an urban life replete with street scuffles but instead has moved up the enlisted chain of command and is seeking one more promotion before putting in for retirement. Like Derek, all of these reservists consciously identified the military as a lifeline out of early predicaments or limited life opportunities. Isaac Greene, for example, "joined the army out of desperation" to escape his dysfunctional and embarrassing urban family. While Luis Balderas did not experience the embarrassment of family, like Isaac and Derek, he grew up in an inner-city environment for which he devised an escape plan.

❖ Luis Balderas

As a muscular man, Luis Balderas may have the physical presence to negotiate the streets of his childhood ghetto, but there is a sweetness to him that makes it difficult to envision him anywhere but a suburban neighborhood playing a pickup game of basketball with the local kids. Few soldiers are as animated in our conversations as Luis: he is a man who loves to tell good stories, and since they are wonderfully informative and entertaining, we happily talked with him for more than two hours. One of the most vivid of the many stories he relates about his life and his experiences is the way in which as an adolescent he devised a plan to use the military as an avenue out of ghetto life:

What drew my attention to the military was at the age of I guess thirteen, I saw a Marines commercial on the TV, and it just caught my eye—the uniform and all that. And then, at the age of thirteen, I knew. I said, "Boy, that's what I want to do." I recall calling the recruiter at age thirteen—"Hey, I want to join the Marines." "Well, how old are you?" "I'm thirteen." "Well, you too young, man. Wait 'til—we'll send you some stuff in the mail, but you know you've gotta wait until you're sixteen with parents' permission or eighteen. You've gotta have a diploma and all that.". . . Here I am in Brooklyn, New York. My friends are selling crack—drugs all over the place, you know. And I'm tryin' to make something positive in a negative environment. I don't want to be here in New York in this environment. I go to work. I come home, and I get nice stuff and then, you know, if I get a nice car, here goes somebody is going to be jealous. They gonna break it. They gonna steal it. They gonna just vandalize it. You know, why go through all that? I've been—it's time for me to just get up, and for me, it was more escapism as well. It was a way out of inner-city life.

As Luis is nearing high school graduation, he is devastated when his older brother usurps his dream and joins the Marines before Luis has the chance to do so. But Luis softens when his brother returns from basic training with some advice about the various military branches and their educational benefits:

[My brother's] home from basic training and stuff, and he's telling me, "No, don't join the Marines." And I'm like, "Well, what're you talkin' about, not joining the Marines?" "Na, join the army instead. They got more money for school. I'm tellin' you. Just listen to me. Join the army, okay." Well, my graduation came up, and it wasn't even a week later I was at the recruiter, at the army recruiter, and signed up.

Luis initially joined the active-duty component of the army after being drawn in by a world that looked impressive, provided strong purpose, helped turn boys into men, and would ultimately lead to a way out of the bleak prospects of inner-city life. After four years in the active component, Luis decided to finish his eight-year contract through service in the reserves. Firmly believing that reserve service would not require much of him other than one weekend a month plus two weeks a year, Luis looked forward to pursing civilian goals.

A Way Up — Reserve Service as Social Mobility

The final pathway to military service involves purely economic calculations on the part of reservists. These recruits use military service to achieve their civilian goals and are drawn to a variety of concrete financial enticements, including educational benefits, training for civilian law enforcement careers, and additional retirement benefits. They view the reserve system as a part-time commitment that will lead to full-time civilian success. College student Kate Arnold, whose father had been an active-duty soldier, joined the Reserve as "an impulsive decision." Her father admonished her for not having thought through the choice more fully, but the easygoing Kate giggles at the irony of joining "mostly [for] college money. That pretty much was my main motive." She pauses, considering this answer, and laughs again—"Well, college money works better when you're actually in college and not deployed." Luke Fisher is equally candid about the importance of drawing on college benefits as he oscillated between feeling the need for military benefits to get ahead in life and making it on his own without joining the military.

❖ Luke Fisher

As Luke Fisher describes the college ambitions that brought him to the Army Reserve, it is easy to picture him maneuvering in a white-collar business world that relies upon quickness of wit, a winning smile, and a hint of calculated charm. Luke is a self-described selfish person, unaccustomed to thinking of the needs of others before joining the military. Now, after eleven years of service, he takes great pride in the leadership he provides enlisted men and women via his position as a junior NCO. Luke likes to joke around a lot and has a bright smile that he flashes as he recalls what prompted him to enlist with the Reserve:

> Commercials. Actually, I just saw money for college—Montgomery GI Bill. . . . I initially tried to join the army in high school, and I was going to go active duty, but I got the scholarships, so I didn't need the military—well, I thought I didn't need the military at the time. So I opted out of joining at that time. . . . But I think I chose the wrong college to go to. It was a lot more expensive than what the scholarships were paying, so I transferred to a smaller college. But then I still didn't have enough money to do what I wanted to do, so it was time to move out of the home. So I was twenty-one when I actually joined the military.

In addition to his scholarship funds running low, Luke found that

> the house was getting small. I was living with my mom, and I have three younger sisters, and one of my younger sisters just had a child, and of course, all of us were living in the house, and my mom has a three-bedroom house. With three sisters, and of course my mom was there, and myself and a baby on the—well, the baby was there by the time I joined—I was like, I gotta go.

The finances of living on his own, being in the Reserve, and trying to go to college never quite worked out for Luke. Like several other soldiers originally motivated to earn educational benefits, Luke's college degree remains unfinished. With mounting family responsibilities through a recent marriage and fatherhood, the financial burden of home life, and a full-time civilian position of which he is relatively fond, it is unlikely that Luke will utilize the educational benefits that he has accrued.

If funding for college is a top motivator for enlistment, positioning oneself for a civilian criminal justice position is a strong second. Like Peter Corell, mentioned earlier in this chapter, more than a third of the 893rd's members are men and women who currently work in civilian criminal justice positions or are training to enter the field. Their civilian expertise spans the local, state, and federal levels of criminal justice.[7] In addition, other soldiers who fully intend to utilize military training as an entry point for the criminal justice field ultimately end up working alternate jobs. Pat Bickford, whose job history includes both factory work and customer service, originally joined the Reserve because "I was looking to get into the law enforcement career and I though it would really help me out with experience." Service in the reserves has enabled some soldiers to pursue civilian law enforcement goals, but for Pat and others, such has not been the case.

Intending to Weave the Military into the Fabric of Civilian Life

Reservists share a sense of national duty with professional soldiers but have identities far more firmly rooted in civilian life.[8] Like so many of his reserve colleagues, Jesse Barnes, a young enlistee from a rural community, reveals his commitment to civilian life. With the 893rd back to the one-weekend-a-month training routine, Jesse is anxious to move on with his civilian goals.

> I don't really think about [the military] at all during that time we're off. When I come back here [to the reserve center], it's, "I got this contract to fill," and you kinda gotta snap back in that military role. . . . I'm more concentrated on a civilian life right now as far as going to school, graduating, and moving on in a civilian career. I only think about this, right now, one weekend a month. And the only time it really sinks in that you're a soldier is, well, of course, active duty and you go on deployments, 'cause then that's your life. But as of right now I'm more concentrated on civilian.

Whether enlisting directly into the Reserve or transferring in from active-duty full-time service, the overwhelming majority of the citizen-soldiers we came to know believe that becoming a reservist differs greatly from joining active duty. They believe the recruiting campaigns that talk of the reserves as a part-time job close to home that helps enable civilian aspirations. Since the reserve system is imagined as requiring only one weekend a month and two weeks a year of training, military duties could be woven into the fabric of civilian lives.[9]

Luis Balderas knows what it means to be a full-time active-duty soldier: he served four years before transferring into the reserve system. He thought he was transferring to a world that would enable him to more fully engage in his family life and pursue a civilian career in corrections. Although he is a happy-go-lucky guy with a generally positive outlook on life, Luis feels no need to conceal his disillusionment with the inconsistency between what he anticipated and what he experienced after joining the Reserve. When asked to relay a story about being a citizen-soldier, Luis takes no time to ponder the question:

I've been deployed twice as a reservist and none as an active member. What's wrong with that picture? That's the end. That's the end. There's people who do this active. I've done [active duty], too, more than willing to—wherever you want me to go, I'll go. Nope? [You haven't deployed me?] Time's up. Wow, I didn't even get nowhere. Okay, well whatever. So much for the awards and homecomings, you know, the experience and all that. Well, here I am as a reservist, and I get called out twice in two years with a four-month break. Wow, what else is next? Do I go active duty? Maybe I'll have a better chance not getting deployed out. . . .

I reenlisted [with the Reserve] right before 9/11. And I recall my words exactly. And if I can grab 'em and put 'em back in my mouth and delete 'em from my memory bank, I would not have said it. But when I signed up, [the recruiter] said, "Sign here, sign here." You know I'm signing my life away. I've been here, done that. Yeah, yeah, whatever, whatever. "Sign here, sign here." I was like, "Ah, well, don't matter. Nothin's going to jump off no time soon." This was August 2001. It wasn't even two weeks later—September 11. I can grab my words back, shove 'em down my throat.

On September 10, 2001, the men and women of the 893rd were situated in a wide variety of civilian life positions—starting college, finishing basic training, starting new jobs, closing in on finishing college, planning to get married, forming new relationships, continuing in long-time jobs, working for the government, working for the private sector, being self-employed, having grown children, having small children, being engaged and active fathers, or having simply fathered children for which they want little responsibility. By in large, they never truly envisioned long-term deployments, particularly to a war zone. While they trained monthly for the possibility of war, they presumed that the use of this training would be limited to police work in the face of national disasters or at special events, such as providing security for the Winter Olympics in Utah. With 9/11 and President Bush's decisions to wage war in both Afghanistan and Iraq, total force policy was finally implemented in its full dress form, and the lives of the reservists of the 893rd and thousands of other citizen-soldiers have changed dramatically, with no clear end in sight.

four

Adaptive Reservists

"I Like Doing What We Do Here"

Now [that we're back from Iraq], being a student is more important to me, and the civilian career, . . . but once we get that call and we are deployed, things just really, other than keeping in good contact with my family, it's kind of just a complete 180, it just becomes an active duty. It's kind of a weird transition, but in my mind-set, it's not very hard. . . . As a reservist, I don't kind of consider myself a soldier. Like the first day of school, we have to go around and everyone gives a little background of themselves. I tell people I'm in the army reserves, but I try not to just say that experience. There's other things I feel tie into my life that are more important. I'm really into baseball. Also, I just want to get along with my civilian career in law enforcement.

Enlisted Army Reservist Zach Bendock

Identity, as Zach Bendock illustrates, is a fluid asset that many reservists draw upon to navigate the incredible complexities of their lives after 9/11. Army Reserve recruiting campaigns emphasize the coequal status of being both a civilian and a soldier. But following 9/11, the military became a very greedy institution, encompassing the lives of those in the 893rd. Operation Noble Eagle put these reservists into a war zone and imposes on them the responsibilities of full-time soldiering, and Zach's comment speaks specifically to his shifting identity from thinking of himself primarily as a citizen to that of a soldier and now reintegrating back into his civilian world.

Zach is a polite young college student. The slight wave to his short, dark hair seems to defy the stiff-topped buzz cuts so prominent in the military, and the sparkle in his eyes when he smiles completes his all-American appearance, which rivals even the most popular young Hollywood actors. When we met up with him several months following his return from Iraq, Zach was one of the first soldiers we interviewed who told us a story that sounded quite different from news accounts of war-torn families and reintegration difficulties. He told us of his loving relationship with his parents; the tremendous support he received from his mother and grandmother throughout his deployments; his slight disappointment in his siblings for having been a bit self-involved during his time away from home; his maturation process since living in the barracks at Ft. McHenry; the closeness he felt to his grandmother following the passing of his grandfather; and his ease and excitement at having gotten back to his college studies and his baseball team. Studies of the aftereffects of wartime soldiering, with their heavy emphasis on psychological and social problems, provided little guidance for interpreting what we heard from Zach.[1] In fact, when asked if his unit's mission had been worth his personal sacrifices, Zach not only answers in the affirmative but eloquently predicts a long conflict in Iraq and references the impact he hopes his service will have on future generations:

> I don't know why they thought it wouldn't take too long, but to get a good democracy government going over there—in the long run it's what they're going to need, but it's going to take so many years probably. I guess it's worth it because we can't have a nation just waging war on others, and with a leader like Saddam especially, and then we can't have terrorism in our country, so maybe my friend's child doesn't have to join the army and deal with somebody like Saddam, so maybe in the long run, the real long run, it will be worth it. For all of us there now, we may not see any benefits to it, other than just being honored by serving.

How had Zach weathered the multiple disruptions to his life with such relative ease? Why did he—and as we would come to find, half of the soldiers with whom we spoke—exhibit such unexpected resiliency? Nothing in Zach's experiences suggests that he is struggling to find a place for himself somewhere within a nebulous space between the civilian world he had left behind and the civilian world that moved on in his absence. Zach and many of his colleagues managed somehow to avoid the pitfalls of civilian reentry about which they had been warned during demobilization classes. Sure, Zach was a little nervous about meeting up with his family when he returned first from Ft. McHenry and subsequently from Iraq, but in each case the awkwardness soon dissipated: he notes, "After a day or two with your family, it seems like everything's changed, but everything's back to where it was." As he explains the changes that took place in his life in the two years following 9/11, Zach focuses on the deployments as positive growth experiences.

> I just realize how important each moment is that you have with your family. Until these deployments I didn't realize—I did, but I didn't try to make each day important. I'm doing a little better thinking through decisions. Better in handling stress a little bit. Deployments help you get closer to your family—at least I did. I don't know, some people that you talk to might be opposite.

Zach and many of his fellow citizen-soldiers negotiate their post-9/11 lives in ways that either minimize the negative impacts of the deployments or yield primarily positive outcomes.

Moving in Lockstep with Institutional Demands

Half of all of the reservists with whom we talked reveal adaptive capabilities that allow them to move from their civilian lives to those of full-time soldiers and then back to their primarily civilian duties and identities. Their transitions began from the time the second airplane hit the Twin Towers, and people across the nation came to realize that the first plane was not a terrible accident but a deliberate attack. Glenn Adams, like many of his colleagues, speaks of the shift in his identity. After two years in the active component of the army, Glenn transferred to the reserves and has spent twenty years proudly serving the country in that capacity. Glenn talks about his transformation from viewing his life primarily as a citizen to embracing his soldier identity:

> Well I love being a soldier. . . . But I would have to admit, back when I did have a regular civilian job before September 11, I would say I was more citizen than soldier, but even then, like I said, there was always something coming up that had to be taken care of. But at this point right now, I'd say as those things hit me at home, I react to 'em almost immediately just because that's the mode I'm in right now. Before it was like, "Okay, I have to get to this, I have to get to that," and so probably before September 11 I was more citizen than soldier, but now it's flip-flopped.

This "flip-flop" of identity from citizen to soldier during the deployments is common among all of the reservists, though the salience of soldier identity dissipates after returning home.[2] Even Glenn, who so proudly identifies himself as a soldier during our conversation, decides to retire from the military several months later.

While Glenn and other adaptive reservists came to identify heavily with being soldiers during their deployments, they do not forgo their civilian ties or identities but instead fold aspects of their civilian lives into being soldiers. They take great pride in drawing on civilian skills in ways that enhance their performance as soldiers or create a better overall environment for the company. Whenever we spoke with the members of the company about what enabled them to keep in contact with their family and friends back home, they frequently referenced the luxury of having a company Internet café jerry-rigged by one of the reservists utilizing his civilian computer skills. Craig McCormick used his civilian training in speech patterns to help break down barriers with the Iraqis and Kuwaitis. As a former active-duty soldier, Craig went into his post-9/11 deployments with a high degree of skepticism about the abilities of his fellow reservists but soon found not only that his civilian skills improved his soldiering but so did those of his fellow reservists.

When I went overseas and we were talking to Iraqi civilians, talking to the Kuwaitis, whoever, I felt more comfortable doing that. I felt very comfortable doing that. Whereas some other people were a little more daunted by that. And by the same token, we have guys here in the unit who are civilian police officers and correction officers who were invaluable over there because they deal with prisoners all the time. And they know how to communicate. They know the roles they have to play. They know how to get a message across. And that's one of the things that really impressed me about the army reservists. . . . When it comes to the military, reservists do things differently because they're not as regimented as active-duty people are. They're much more likely to sit down with their commanding officer and say, "Hey, sir, you shouldn't do this. This is not—let's do it this way." They're much more likely to kind of question the orders or at least if not directly question them, say, "Yes, sir, but let's try this instead." Or make a suggestion. Whereas people on active duty are more likely to say, "Yes, sir." Turn around and think, "This is wrong. This is messed up. This is stupid. But I'm going to do it." So, from what I've seen, like I said in the reserves, over there, the civilian skills that people brought were more of a benefit—or at least their benefit outweighed the lack of military bearing or discipline that some people might bring.

The adaptive reservists of the 893rd do not give up their civilian ways as they become more heavily aligned within their soldiering duties but instead allow their identities to ebb and flow as situations call for a greater emphasis in one area or another. What enables them to be resilient as the military weighs heavily on them and danger becomes a way of life?

Adaptive Qualities

When taken as a group, adaptive soldiers share five qualities that contribute to their markedly resilient handling of multiple deployments. They have strong civilian networks that pick up the slack in their absence and enable home life to operate relatively smoothly in their absence. Everyone who came to the reserves having already served an international deployment as an active-duty soldier falls into the adaptive cluster, although not all members of the group had such service abroad. Also, adaptive soldiers kept what turned out to be very realistic expectations about the possibility of multiple deployments. While some reservists lulled themselves into believing that the deployment to Ft. McHenry would fulfill their role as soldiers in the U.S. Army Reserve, adaptive soldiers worked at preparing themselves, their families, and those under their command for the distinct possibility of an overseas deployment. As for politics, adaptive soldiers support the Bush administration's decision to invade Iraq and overturn Saddam Hussein's regime. Regardless of a lack of evidence of Saddam's possession of weapons of mass destruction, adaptive soldiers believe that U.S. military involvement in Iraq is warranted. Finally, adaptive soldiers take great pride in their service to the military and to the nation.

Quality of Social Networks

Seth Walker is an easygoing college student who proposed to his girlfriend between deployments and is now looking forward to their upcoming wedding. Throughout his two deployments, she and his parents completely supported his needs, and he points to their support in easing his life since 9/11.

> I guess I just have to say that family is like a big thing, and when you're gone, I think it's really important to have them there for you. I think you can tell like on a personal level that, like, certain individuals who have close family and [those who] don't, they react differently to certain situations. . . . I think if you have someone to rely back on— I know there's a couple people that had their wife cheating on them or their wife wanted to leave, and you could just tell those people were miserable because of that. It didn't help the situation. Like, I always knew everything at home was good. I knew my—if something would happen to my fiancée, my parents would be there for her. Or if something would happen to my parents, I knew my brother, my sister, and my fiancée would be there. So I always knew someone was there for the other person to take care of. I knew, with me being gone, it wasn't the end of their world, they could still survive.

Several adaptive reservists have social support networks that not only run deep within their families but cut across the many spheres of their civilian lives. Craig McCormick and his family are among the reservists steeped in a community ready to lend a helping hand.

❖ Craig McCormick

When Craig McCormick was called to Iraq, he left behind his pregnant wife and their three children, but he took comfort in knowing that his family was receiving an outpouring of support from a host of church and community members. When asked who was most supportive of his deployments, he exclaimed,

> Everybody! I mean from the word *go*. From 9/11 on until the unit deployed and even after that, the first words out of everybody's mouth was "What can we do?" Coworkers, people at church, neighbors, everybody—"Tell me what to do. What can we do?" We had a million phone numbers of, "Tell your wife she can call me if she needs this. I can watch the kids. I can make dinner. I can everything." So other than the immediate family members, everybody was supportive. I mean, people were coming out of the woodwork. . . . After a while it gets to the point where we don't really need anything. Life—you can handle life, as she was a single parent in many ways, and people can do that. And so she didn't have to call on a lot of people for support. Sometimes it came out of the blue. I have a coworker whose husband has a landscaping company and my wife said something to somebody about the shrubs in the garden or something, and two days later this guy brought his crew over and they did the whole house, and she didn't even know they were coming. Things like that would happen. So all the needs were taken care of.

Craig also speaks of the ways in which his relationships, particularly with his wife, have been strengthened through his deployments to Ft. McHenry and then later to Iraq.

> We both became better communicators, though it's because we had to. It wasn't the situation where, okay, I know I'm going to be with my

wife every day and we can figure out each other's moods by body language or action or anything like that. It was, we had to talk about problems and hopes and fears and worries. We had to talk through it all. So, that helped us a lot. It really helped both of us. I know it did me. . . . You have to be—you have to actively engage yourself in the family in ways that you wouldn't have to if you were there all the time. So it's, it can be beneficial. *For me anyway.* Obviously, for some people, it could be hard for them. There are situations where the husband is removed from the family for a period of time, for deployment, and he uses that as license to go out and do whatever—his wife, too. So there, that, maybe those relationships were doomed from the start. But for some people, I can see it's not always obviously going to be a positive experience. But we've certainly made, I don't know, the expression making gold out of straw or whatever. We've turned it into a positive thing—lemonade out of lemons.

While stories of widespread civilian support are common among the adaptive soldiers, these men and women also express disappointment in the media's portrayal of the military's involvement in Iraq. Craig juxtaposes the personal support he received with what he perceives as a lack of support from the news media or general population.

Again, personal level, I got all the support. I wish—not I wish, but it would have been nice, I think, if people had supported what we were doing a little bit more. Especially—and that's what I would talk about when I called home and I would say, "Okay, this is maybe what you've seen on CNN or read in *Newsweek,* but let me tell you, I read that *Newsweek* article, too, and I'm sitting right here, and what that guy wrote was not accurate, was not true, and let me tell you about these kids I was talking to on the street the other day. And let me tell you about this unit down the road that just built a new police station and just repaired the hospital and just rebuilt an amusement park kind of thing. This is—these are the benefits that people are getting." And so I'm kinda pitching the "let's be a little more supportive of the whole war effort or rebuilding effort" with people. And that would have been nice, and just generally it'd be nice if people would see that.

Home support in all of its various forms had tremendous importance to all of the men and women who remained adaptive throughout
the multiple deployments and demobilization processes. Transitioning
into the full-time role of soldier is certainly less problematic when loved
ones at home also transition into thinking of the reservists in their lives
as full-time soldiers performing necessary national defense rather than
as civilians forced into unreasonably long deployments. Adaptability is
intimately linked to having family, friends, and community members
who respond to the call to active duty with strong support in all its
forms. From what may seem like the simplest act of sending a letter or
a small care package to willingly taking on full-time responsibilities for
raising children and running households, home support is a shared
experience of all adaptive soldiers, whether young or old, male or
female, married or single.

Prior Active-Duty Deployment Experience

Many of the adaptive reservists shared another experience. All those
reservists who initially joined the military as full-time active-duty personnel and served at least one deployment outside the United States are
among the most adaptive citizen-soldiers. Prior active-duty deployment
experience is not a requirement for navigating the multiple deployments with few difficulties, however. Zach Bendock, for example, is
among the adaptive reservists who joined the Reserve straight out of
high school and never saw a military base outside of the contiguous
United States prior to 9/11. Every reservist with whom we spoke who
had at least one international deployment with the regular army—in
Germany, Cuba, Panama, Bosnia, Korea, or any other place of U.S. military involvement—weathered his or her post-9/11 deployments in part
by drawing on previous deployment experiences.[3] In contrast, none of
those reservists who were less adaptive to the post-9/11 events and
deployments had active-duty deployment experience. Several of them
had served under the active-duty component, but their service was limited to bases in the contiguous United States.

As a former active-duty soldier who spent several years on deployment rotations during his early twenties, junior NCO Sam Kriner is the most experienced member of the 893rd MP Company in terms of deployments and has served, among other places, in Bosnia, Somalia, and Egypt and in Saudi Arabia during the first Gulf War. Sam transferred to the reserves about six years ago to live a more family-friendly life, but he and his wife remained well equipped through their experiences to handle the news of the company's deployment to Ft. McHenry. They had already been separated during the birth of his first child while he served a rotation in Cuba and over the years have learned a great deal about what works for them when it comes to raising a family in the midst of deployments. For example, when he is home, Sam is the self-described "punisher" of the children, and with his deep voice, it is easy to imagine a tone that surely makes his three boys stop whatever they are up to and take notice. However, when Sam is away on deployments, he backs off of that role, opting instead to let the children know that he supports his wife's disciplinary decisions. Although Vince Stephenson shares some of the same characteristics as Sam—in his early thirties, having served deployments as an active-duty soldier, and of a similar NCO rank—as a single man, he does not need to worry about a wife and children while on deployments. Even without a family to worry about, however, Vince talks a good deal about the many lessons he has learned during prior deployments—particularly financial mistakes he made along the way—and how he shares his experiences with younger soldiers.

❖ Vince Stephenson

About a year prior to 9/11, Vince Stephenson decided to transition out of being a full-time soldier and into the Reserve. He "was going for a change in lifestyle and wanted to get some college in." Ever the pragmatist, he got a job with a national lumberyard chain in hopes of having a schedule that could accommodate college courses. He was not completely certain what he wanted to study, but unlike most members of the 893rd, he wanted nothing to do with law enforcement in civilian life, although he had been an MP throughout his professional soldiering days. Although Vince had been moving toward transitioning out of soldiering, the attacks on the World Trade Center brought him almost instantly back to a soldier's life. Vince, who reveals little about what he feels, talks in almost a mechanical way about his active-duty deployments and how he learned through his mistakes to minimize the impact of these reserve deployments. He runs his fingers through his short, stiff hair and explains with an air of confidence,

> I've deployed before, in active duty. I've been to Panama, Cuba. I spent a year overseas in Hawaii, and then I came home stateside and finished out in Virginia. . . . I've done it before. My family's used to it. We—I learned the hard way in Panama, what to do, what not to do, finances. I went that route, and it cost me a lot, and so my family is my support when I leave. We have it all set up. And before I went to Ft. McHenry, I just sit down with my parents, explain, "Here's all the bills. This is what I've done." Get my mother set up so she can run it her way, her system. And my father, my computer, e-mails, teaching him how to use the Internet, 'cause that's obviously now's a new form of communication 'cause phone calls are rather expensive. . . . You start calling from Panama to home, and not knowing the ins and outs, I had about a thousand-dollar phone bill in the first month. And when you're a private, you don't make a whole lot of money, so cut that out real quick and you start to learn the military has the DSL lines and you can call from post to post and then it's a local call from . . . the closest installation. You start to learn that real quick.

Vince's pragmatism comes through as he reflects on the possibility of a third post-9/11 deployment with the 893rd:

> And coming back from this, from Iraq, if I'm home past New Year's, I'm happy. And they yank me next year in 2005, it's not gonna hurt me. I just know, bodies are short. You gotta pull from somewhere, so, I mean, I'm prepared mentally.

Having a background that includes a deployment with the active component of the military helps these seasoned reservists navigate what for greener reservists is the unfamiliar territory of being away from home in a military capacity.

Realistic Expectations about Multiple Deployments

When the members of the 893rd left for Ft. McHenry within a month of 9/11, their initial orders suggested that they should be prepared to be stationed at Ft. McHenry for up to two years. The word came down later through the ranks that their mission would likely be closer to a year. The question arose as to what was next for them, and rumors flew throughout their time at Ft. McHenry. The United States was well into the invasion of Afghanistan, and while the Taliban regime had been dispersed, the hunt for Osama bin Laden remained a top priority. Negotiations with Saddam Hussein were also escalating into threats of an invasion in search of weapons of mass destruction. While many reservists lulled themselves into believing that their deployment to Ft. McHenry fulfilled their obligation to what they hoped would be a grateful nation, the adaptive soldiers held what turned out to be much more realistic ideas about the potential for additional deployment. After returning home from Ft. McHenry, they turned their attention toward preparing themselves, their families, and any soldiers under them in the company chain of command for the likelihood of another deployment. Lane Wright explains that those with their eyes open

> saw it comin'. Obviously there was—rumors flew around every month, and they—the whole five months [between deployments], every month's drill leading into was, they just kept stressin' that we were going to go again, and to the point where you knew they weren't just rumors or they weren't just tryin' to scare us. And then when they started givin' us anthrax shots, that shot isn't exactly cheap. They don't give it out for no reason at all. So it softened the blow a lot.

Like many of the college students within the company, Kate Arnold, whose studies had been interrupted by the Ft. McHenry deployment, reenrolled in college for the spring semester. While a number of the college students were hoping to be able to knock out at least one more full semester before being called for a second deployment, Kate is a realist, even laughing at the futility of trying to remain in school as the tensions with Iraq mounted:

As we were coming home—it was when the whole Iraq thing was really starting to fire up—and we all knew, okay, we're going to go to Iraq. We just didn't know when. So it was kind of, well, I'm going to come home and enjoy my break, but waiting to go there. I started school again. I knew it was pointless, but give it a shot. So it was just nice to have a break from army stuff even though I knew I was going to have to go back. [The news of the Iraq deployment] wasn't so much of a shock 'cause like I said, it was every drill we came back from there, it was "Get ready. Get ready." It was just a matter of when is the phone call going to happen. So it was just kind of, "Hey, everybody, it happened." So we all kind of knew it was going to, so it was more of a, "Okay, let's accept this and get it over with."

Supportive of the War

In his book *No Victory Parade,* historian and essayist Murray Polner draws on interviews with returning Vietnam War veterans who struggled to reenter a civilian world after an unpopular war. Polner's depiction of the veterans includes those he dubbed hawks and doves. The hawks tended to support military efforts in general, even if they struggled with atrocities witnessed in Vietnam. Doves, some of whom went to Vietnam with a promilitary attitude, came home more committed to ending the war through collective action. Although all of the reservists of the 893rd support the military enough to have volunteered for one weekend a month and two weeks a year drill training, within the company, their level of support of the Bush administration's actions in the "global war on terrorism" certainly differ. Many of the adaptive soldiers are the strongest supporters of the Bush administration and believe that something needed to be done to bring down Iraqi dictator Saddam Hussein. While very broad support comes from Laura Stutzman, who explains, "I think anytime you're called out for the military, no matter what, it is, it's worth it," most soldiers speak more narrowly about the mission at hand in Iraq and the positive events they witnessed. Vince Stephenson explains the importance of removing Saddam Hussein from power:

I know everybody else has their political views of why we should be there, not be there. But in dealing and talking with the Iraqi people, I mean, you can see the effects that Saddam Hussein has had on them and his punishment regards. I mean, we had kids in our facility, and they're out looting, stealing. We picked them up, but some of these kids under Saddam's regime, you do something wrong like [stealing], they took a finger. And this one kid had three fingers missing. And so when you get that part of the story—and that's the stuff that they don't put on TV—and realize, yeah, weapons of mass destruction, we found it, didn't find it, but when you look at the people and what they have had to endure over some of the other, other individuals that might of had to work for Saddam or in the Republican Guard or whatever. If they didn't, he'd kill their family, kill them, so, I mean, it's you gotta make a choice, and if it's to keep your family safe, then you're gonna do what you have to do. . . . That's my views on it. Yes, I mean, it was worthwhile being there.

Junior NCO and political conservative Lane Wright feels that it is inappropriate for soldiers to question the larger military mission, but he may find it easier to adhere to this claim because he strongly supports President George W. Bush's efforts in Iraq and Afghanistan.

I'm a pretty conservative Republican type, so I just get tired of Bush bashing. That's the only thing. I would rather them—I would rather not hear. And I've really been on the liberal media lately, too, that's my kick. I'm probably watching too much Bill O'Reilly, but I would rather not hear anything than [hear] the bashing. Because my philosophy has always been, you're told to do something, you do it, as far as military's concerned. I don't—the politics behind the war, I don't care one bit about. I'm told to go, I go. Told to do a job, I do it and proud to.

And it's like the whole [2004 presidential candidate John] Kerry thing right now, they talk about him coming home from the war and that's one thing I don't like about him a lot. It seems like he came home from the war and just turned his back on his military roots, and I'd call it stabbed 'em in the back, which there's a term other people are using, too, but I don't believe in that. Even if—I know Vietnam was a terrible thing too, not a war like this. But I just believe you don't bad-mouth the—how do I put it into words? It's like stickin' to the party line even if it's not your party. Do you know what I mean? So that's the only thing gets to me. And I used to get on a couple of friends of mine that are more liberal Democratic type that were in Iraq with me that are dear friends of mine. That they would [say], "Why are we here? This is stupid. Bush this and that." I'd say, "Hey, look, you're here. It's not your room, your part to say anything. You just do your job." So that's the only thing that gets to me.

Support of military action did not mean support of dishonorable action by military personnel. The news about the Abu Ghraib prison and military police reserve soldiers' involvement in the torture of Iraqi prisoners there certainly casts a shadow of suspicion on the activities of all reserve soldiers, most especially MP reservists. While the soldiers of the 893rd have varying reactions to Abu Ghraib, enlistee Laura Stutzman expresses a common level of anger toward the soldiers involved in the torture. When asked whether the events surrounding the prison abuse scandal have affected the way people view her, Laura's frustration with the situation comes through loud and strong:

That's the first thing, like when people find out I'm a soldier and then they find out that I'm an MP, they're like, "Did you know those people, or what do you think of that?" I think what every other red-blooded American thinks. It's disgusting. Like—and I didn't know any of them. Like I feel that I have to go through that every time. Almost defending myself each time. I mean, that one girl, she wasn't even an MP, and that's another thing they keep messing up on the news. That she was a clerk. But, yeah, that's frustrating 'cause you go over there and you think you do this like really good job, and you're proud of what you did, and then you come home, and it's just like thrown in your face. Like we're still getting talks about it. . . . So it's frustrating just because a small group of people messed up.

For the members of the 893rd, the ability to differentiate their company's behavior from that of the individuals involved in the reported abuses is important to maintaining pride in their accomplishments.

Pride in a Job Well Done

When the adaptive reservists speak of their national service, they tend to radiate pride regarding their time while deployed.[4] When Darnell Powell joined the reserves in the mid-1990s, during his freshman year of college, he was not looking for money to help pay for college—he already had a scholarship for that. He was looking for an "adventure," "something out of the ordinary." While he works in a subdued white-collar job, in his spare time, Darnell loves thrill-seeking activities: "I learned how to skydive. I ride a motorcycle. I love snowboarding. . . . I don't like to say this, but, see, I'm from D.C., so a lot of people from D.C. don't do this type of thing." His service with the 893rd has certainly brought about several thrilling moments. As Darnell explains what being a citizen-soldier means to him, he captures the feelings expressed by many of his colleagues about the level of commitment needed to be a reservist or professional soldier after 9/11.

> It's just like going beyond being a regular citizen. It shows almost your dedication, like I don't regret going to Ft. McHenry, I don't regret going to Iraq. If I gotta go to Iraq again, I would have to. Because I know it's for a cause, and it's for a purpose, and it's that dedication that sets you aside. Because a lot of people, they probably wouldn't want to join the military now 'cause, like my, a big—well, I really admire [Pat] Tillman, the [NFL] football player that dropped everything to [join the U.S. Army]. So it's like you make—you're in your high-life career and everything, and he dropped everything to join the military for dedication for a cause, and that's sort of like how I feel about it, too. Like, I did this in the beginning just for the fun, but now I support it more, and, I mean, I really respect what I do, and anybody else that's in the military and reserves that lay their life down for a purpose and a cause for your country.

The pride in going the extra mile and having proven oneself through service in Iraq came up several times in our interview with Laura Stutzman, a young enlisted soldier enrolled in college in hopes of following her father into a law enforcement career.

❖ Laura Stutzman

Laura was in basic training during the 893rd's Ft. McHenry deployment and subsequently assigned to the company after its return from stateside deployment. Since Iraq was her first and so far only deployment, she remains eligible and willing to serve another. As such, when she speaks of the importance of being a soldier rather than a citizen, she does so while remaining keenly aware that she may at any time be called for an additional extended deployment. When asked about the meaning of being a citizen-soldier, Laura's already infectious smile widens as she beams with pride in having shown herself capable of extraordinary service to the country.

> It makes up who you are after a while. I don't know. I really love it. I guess it introduces you to what you're made of and who you really are. Something I'm really proud [of], and I really like doin' it. So I guess that would be like the best way to sum it up. . . . Different things, like I guess you'd be surprised like what kinda stuff you can do when you're, like, put in a situation that you wouldn't normally be put in. I don't know. I don't know how to explain it well. You really know what you're made of after you do it.

Laura's pride in her service was deepened by having proven herself not only as a citizen-soldier but as a female soldier in a male-dominated military institution carrying out a mission in a country she sees as devaluing women's strength and independence. A striking young woman with intense eyes, Laura endured sexually harassing statements as she worked hard to be taken seriously in her position as an MP prison guard with all the rights and responsibilities of the position.

> [Being a female soldier] was difficult to an extent because for the longest time [the prisoners] didn't want to listen to me because—I assume because I am a female. . . . Then you've gotta get to a point where you have to show them, like, you are in charge, and they're gonna listen to you. And that's frustrating. And then there were a lot of men there, especially the ones that spoke English, that just only

look at you like as a thing, a sex thing. Like, I had a man there ask me to be his mistress. I mean, of course they already have like a million wives, and then another man was like, "Will you marry me?" Like, dead serious. Like, wanted to know how he could get in touch with me after we got home. So that's—yeah, that's one thing, and you can't change that.

I mean, no matter, it's a hard thing to deal with when you're a female over there because they have no respect, and I don't know. That definitely made me angry. I'll take that with me probably until I die because that, I mean, that was every day for like seven months. You had to show them, "I'm in charge, you're gonna listen to me, blah, blah, blah." So that was not fun. I also—I know this sounds awful, but I don't respect their way of life at all, like, just from that. That disgusts me. I think it shows, like, I don't know, how would you say—that shows a civilized country. If you can respect your women as equals, you're civilized. I mean, they couldn't, no matter what. They treat their dogs better than they treat their mothers over there, so that's frustrating. That's one thing that got to me over there all the time. And it wasn't just like one man—it's like you could have up to a hundred in a cage at one time and you're tryin' to explain to them that you're in charge. . . . I mean, I'm really proud of [my Iraqi service]. Like I really—I don't know. I guess I can say like I'm a really proud person now. I don't know how else you would describe that. . . .

The men over there, how they hate women. Oh, I get so frustrated when I'm somewhere [now], and, like, a man doesn't show me courtesy or whatever, and I'm not talking about opening every door, but I don't know—he looks at me the wrong way or whistles. I mean, that just makes me lose my mind. And I just got back from defending you. So, there goes the pride, too, but I can't stand disrespect for females now. It drives me crazy because, I mean, for the seven months we were over there, that's all we got.

When Laura thinks back over her time in Iraq, she weaves together her strong sense of pride in policing incarcerated Iraqi males with a portrayal of their chauvinistic attitude toward her and her view that Iraqi culture degrades females. The challenges she faced in Iraq have awakened her to an intolerance of male mistreatment that Laura has carried with her back to the States. Juxtaposed with her budding feminist views is the fact that Laura is the only one of her female colleagues who has taken the time to apply noticeable makeup for their drill weekend. While she has learned to negotiate well within this male institution, she has done so while continuing to display her femininity.

Laura also took pride in the signs she got from Iraqi children when she was on prisoner escort missions, taking their gestures as indications of an underlying support among Iraqi youth for the American military invasion.

> I guess seeing like the little kids, like, how much they support us over there. Like when we would go out on missions—like most of the time we'd stay where the prison was, but there were different times when we would have to, like, escort convoys and do things like that. But when we would go out into the town, I mean, little kids would be like running after the Humvee—I mean, just waiving, not asking for anything, giving us thumb's up. They know "Good." That is one American word that they would always say—"Good, good." I don't know. That right there tells me that what we're doing is right. And I think really if we could just keep up with that, I mean, this is a whole generation right here, and this could be what saves our relationship with the Middle East if we could just keep what we have going with those little kids right now. So, that—yeah, that stands out in my mind mostly.

As Laura's story suggests, the pride of these adaptive reservists comes not only from within—in Laura's case, from having proven herself capable of handling incarcerated male Iraqis—but also from positive affirmations from Iraqi civilians, particularly children, early in the war. In addition to drawing on prideful memories of Iraq, adaptive reservists, like the young enlisted Randy Stires, also tell stories of being positively received by community members after returning home.

❖ Randy Stires

As a young boy, Randy Stires dreamed of being the Lone Ranger, a cowboy action hero, or a soldier. As he talks about growing up playing war in the woods behind his house, its easy to picture him as a chubby-cheeked little boy with a toy rifle and soldier helmet, seeking victory in pretend battles fought with his friends. Now, in his early twenties and having spent the past two years actively soldiering, he is pleasantly surprised at the respect and support his veteran status affords him from his boss and customers.

> Since I've been home, there's a lot of people that have been nothing but nice to me. My boss, my manager, he occasionally goes out on jobs with me, when I work for an extermination company. . . . My boss somehow always winds up talking about it. 'Cause it's like he's so proud to have a veteran working for him. He's like, "Yeah, he just got back from Iraq." A lot of people are like, "Oh, really? That's great. I'm glad you made it back." And they always wind up giving me a tip. I never knew people would get a tip for being an exterminator. Some people give you tips and everything for it. Some guys, they're veterans, too, and they're like, "I know what you mean. We got to quit messing around. We seriously got to fight this war. We can't keep just policing." They always just want to try and talk about that.

Having come of age in the 1940s during the all-encompassing events of World War II, Randy's grandparents are especially proud of him, and Randy notes this as a common theme among the older generation: "A lot of people in that age category are like all, 'Yeah, it's the right thing to do. A young man should be in the military.'"

The positive reinforcement from his family, his boss, and customers contributes to his pride in his soldier status, and coupled with this pride is the fact that being a soldier gives Randy a strong sense of purpose that he sees as lacking in the civilian world.

> The way the army does things is the way I see a lot of people should handle their lives anyways, you know. It's sort of like coming back— it was weird because when I was over there, I thought we had a purpose. But then when coming back, it's like the only purpose is really the work for money, right? But I like the work, so it's sort of funny that I come back and the company I work for, a lot of other guys they're like—I don't want to say a cussword—they're like half-assin'

the job. But me, it's like I just work and I like to have an objective and work for it. And a lot of people, they don't do that. . . . A lot of people—seems like the civilian world, citizens are not really working towards anything. They are not working towards anything, they're just working to work, because it's something you do. . . . They are not worried about anything other than getting that paycheck.

Like Laura Stutzman, Randy remains eligible for another deployment since he transferred into the 893rd just before the company's mobilization to Iraq. Now that he has had the experience of soldiering full time, Randy is seriously considering pursuing his childhood dream and transferring to the army's active-duty component.

Adaptability ≠ No Troubles

Half of the reservists we came to know exhibit resiliency in relation to the seismic changes in their post-9/11 lives. This is not the same as saying that every moment of their mobilization, deployment, and demobilization process went smoothly. For example, while Laura Stutzman describes herself as overall being the same person who went to Iraq, she initially experienced some reintegration problems common to many reservists and professional soldiers alike; however, like her fellow adaptive colleagues, Laura's adjustment issues lasted only a short time.

> It was a little bit difficult, like little things. Like, once I went to the mall with my family, and it was really crowded, and it felt like that wouldn't have bothered me before, but it kinda weirded me out. I was always like lookin' around. I guess I noticed, like, rudeness more, like somebody kinda stepped in front of my mom, and she stumbled a little bit, and I just wanted to be like, "What's wrong with you?" I mean, you're kinda like, I don't want to say ready to fight, but, I mean, you're all like wound up when you're over there, and then you come home, and you're still like that for a while. There is, like, little things, and [they] really get on your nerves. So that was kinda hard. . . .
> I was just really trying to get back to what I loved before, like being a girl again and do the makeup stuff and everything, but, I mean, at the same time I didn't want to go out because there was too

much going on in December. Christmas season—that was the worst. Just because everything's crowded, you go to a restaurant, and you've got to wait, and you're crowded in the stores. . . .

The prison was a little crowded—I mean, you don't ever want somebody behind your back when you're in a prison. And when you go out to the mall, like everyone's behind you. You can't see what's going on around you all the time. I don't know what it really was. I mean, like, I'm fine now, but yeah, I just didn't like the crowds before. . . .

I don't really have patience that much any more. And I don't know how that happened and when it went away or whatever, but my patience has really diminished since I'm back. Like that thing with the crowds in the mall and people being rude, but I really try to keep that out of my family life now, as much as I can.

Vince Stephenson's difficulty was not the emotional adjustment Laura recalls but a frustration in working with his civilian employer to make sure he receives the rights and benefits to which he is legally entitled as a reservist.

My employer—I had to go round and round with my human resources person to get my pay raises because I was entitled to 'em. I know I was entitled to 'em. I had the letter of the law, and I was not gracefully received and pretty much blown off. And I kept raising a stink and brought it up to the, like I said, chain of command, up to the next level, and I took it up to my store manager, and he got on her and said, "No, you will call corporate payroll and figure this out." 'Cause it's something that they just don't know. And there are several soldiers deployed out of my store, and hopefully I'm being the guinea pig so when these guys come back, hopefully they won't have the same problems.

Vince knew that he was entitled to the raises his civilian coworkers received while he was overseas and persistently claimed those benefits even in the face of substantial resistance. Likewise, college student Kate Arnold's primary problem stemmed from being caught between institutional policies that have left her without health insurance. She pushes aside a strand of blond hair and explains her situation:

It's just little difficulties that you don't anticipate. I mean, I guess, for instance, on my twenty-third birthday, I was dropped from my parents' insurance. And being a college student without a full-time job or anything, now I kind of sit here without any health benefits, which is kinda scary because if something happens, then I'm really screwed. But it's little kinda things like that. I tried writing to my congressman, and nothing really seemed to happen with that. I probably should follow it up. But it's tiny little things like that, and it's different, and it kind of in a way doesn't seem fair. But there is nothing really that you can do about it except try and make it different for the future.

The "pick yourself up by the bootstraps" attitude that both Vince and Kate exhibit is common among the adaptive soldiers as they encounter their individual problems. Several entrepreneurs lost their self-owned businesses, one soldier experienced a severe adverse health reaction to an overdose of the required anthrax shots, some children of reservists—particularly young adolescents—had difficulty with their fathers' absences, and the transition out of the adrenaline-laden Iraq environment even brought about a short period of impotence for one married soldier. But these adaptive reservists overwhelmingly feel that their missions at Ft. McHenry and in Iraq have been worth the personal sacrifices.

These reservists say the army's decompression process trained them to expect short-term problems associated with reintegrating into civilian life and that they have coped with the brief difficulties they have encountered. They think of themselves as relatively unchanged save for two points. First, they are more appreciative of the many joys of life, from running water to the love of family and friends. At the same time, they are now less patient or tolerant of what they perceive as inept civilian behaviors. In talking about the positive ways in which his relationship with his wife has grown through the deployment, Keith Jackson notes this common difficulty with a lack of patience/tolerance:

[Our relationship's] gotten closer. A whole lot closer. A lot more understandable for me. For me, with my wife and certain members of my family that really know me and are close to me, they say I don't have patience. They really got to understand after this, believe it or not—I explain to them that it's not that I don't have patience—and this is how I've always been—but going to Baghdad helped me to explain it even better is that I don't have tolerance. I don't have tolerance for repetitious, redundancy stuff. I don't have tolerance to continue with people that should know better that continue to do it and saying it ain't wrong, you know. I can't counsel you. I don't have tolerance to keep counseling you on the same thing that you want to continue. If you want to continue your mess, then, fine, continue it, but don't keep coming to me with that same problem. I don't have tolerance for that.

These soldiers have learned that life is too short to sweat the little stuff. Their new world perspective can put them at odds with a civilian population often caught up in the minutiae of non-life-threatening personal crises.

Coming home also involves a decision process for adaptive reservists. Not obligated to a primary life of soldiering for the time being, these reservists have several options in front of them. Some have come to enjoy soldiering so much that they contemplate transferring to the active-duty component of the army, as in the case of Randy Stires:

I'm not really sure what I want to do. That's why it's sort of hard sometimes, like to say things about myself. . . . I like being in the army. I thought about going active duty—pretty much every day since I've been off of active duty, I have been thinking about going back, not as a reservist but as active duty.

But most of the resilient soldiers decide to reenter a life as citizen-soldiers, emphasizing their identity squarely in the civilian world rather than the military institution. Seth Walker, who is now quite happy to be back home planning his wedding and reenrolling in college with hopes of becoming a teacher, is looking forward to the return of his life as a citizen-soldier:

Now I consider myself more a citizen. . . . I'm proud to have done what I have done. . . . I've done more things than people my age will probably do in the next ten years of their life. I'm behind in school by three and a half years. But I think I came out of it a better person from what I've learned, and I've grown because of it. . . . Looking back on [the deployments] now, it's a lot better in hindsight. And I don't think I'd change the times for anything. I mean, wouldn't give a million bucks for it. I mean, I forget where I read that you couldn't pay 'em a million bucks to go again, but they wouldn't take a million bucks to give up what they had. It was incredible. . . . Now [that I'm back], I only put the uniform on once a month, and I try not to think about it while I'm at home because I've done my time, I feel. I just do my once-a-month for now.

Making Adaptability Visible

War, in part, produces damaged soldiers. The research literature on veterans' experiences with war, most of which has been conducted in the post-Vietnam era, is dominated by the examination of the ways in which wartime soldiering contributes to family disruption and divorce, violence, and most especially mental illness.[5] The cinematic imagery of struggling soldiers returning from war looms large in our collective conscious. The return of sixteen million World War II veterans was accompanied by films such as *The Best Years of Our Lives,* in which three veterans struggled to reconnect with their families lest the war represent the "best years of their lives." The war's lingering effects were also chronicled in the 1956 film *The Man in the Grey Flannel Suit,* in which Gregory Peck portrays an upstanding family man hampered by war flashbacks and the unexpected news that he fathered a child while stationed in Italy. While the 1970s hit television show *M*A*S*H* originally focused on the zany antics of a Korean War mobile military hospital, the show increasingly moved to examine the casualties of war and the cost to service personnel's psychological and physical well-being. In the 1989 blockbuster biographical film *Born on the Fourth of July,* Tom Cruise portrayed Ron Kovic, a patriotic young man who eagerly enlists to fight in Vietnam but comes home paralyzed and finds new meaning in his life through his work as a spokesman for the anti-war movement.

The 1991 Gulf War also sparked Hollywood portrayals of fictional and nonfictional experiences of soldier reentry. The 1996 fictional film *Courage Under Fire* takes as its subject the internal investigation of the appropriateness of posthumously awarding medical helicopter pilot Captain Karen Walden the Congressional Medal of Honor. In addition to the loss of Captain Walden's and several other young soldiers' lives in Iraq, the film depicts Gulf War veterans who come home from the desert and struggle with the demons the war has produced for them. One veteran wrestles with flashbacks, another has become a drug addict, and a third is shown committing suicide as he drives his car into an oncoming train. In 2005, amid the current wars in Iraq and Afghanistan, the movie *Jarhead* was released. This film follows the real-life psychological struggles of marine sniper Anthony Swofford and his company members as they wait in the Saudi desert for wartime combat action that is ultimately denied to them. Swofford's story shows not only that combat can have devastating affects on soldiers' lives but also that the absence of engaging an enemy in battle is equally traumatic for Swofford and his closest colleague.

Most recently, documentaries show returning veterans from the Iraq War struggling to deal with war-induced stress. In the 2006 independent film *When I Came Home,* Iraq war veteran Herold Noel struggles with posttraumatic stress disorder (PTSD) that leaves him a homeless man living out of his car in Brooklyn. *The War Tapes,* also released in 2006, is the first documentary filmed by soldiers as they chronicle their Iraq deployment experiences. The film focuses on three Army National Guardsmen and their New Hampshire–based company. After returning home, Sergeant Steve Pink is diagnosed with PTSD, and specialist Mike Moriarty suffers from severe back and hand pain developed in conjunction with his Iraq duties.

These stories that chronicle the troubles soldiers bring home from war are heartbreaking and demand to be told. That they are retold after—and now during—each war illustrates some of the consequences of war experiences, and the military should make every effort to minimize the psychological and physical injuries of war. But as media and news accounts of returning veterans focus on those with severe mental or physical disabilities, the experiences of those who remain adaptive are overshadowed—or worse, negated. Stories of adaptability also need to be heard, recognized, and understood.[6]

It is harder to see the veterans among us who return from war and go about their lives without visible physical or psychological injuries. While corporations, universities, factories, and small businesses are filled with veterans who bear few outward differences from the civilians around them, their stories are missing from the larger cultural landscape. Adaptability lacks the dramatic tension needed for a blockbuster Hollywood movie. Resiliency is a harder antiwar message around which to rally in support of bringing home the troops. The cost of war in terms of lives lost, physical injuries sustained, and damage to the psyches should never be forgotten. By the middle of 2007, the United States had sustained more than 28,000 wounded soldiers and more than 4,050 deaths in the wars in Iraq and Afghanistan. Although the U.S. government has never collected official figures, the Iraqi Health Ministry estimates that as many as 150,000 Iraqi civilians, police officers, and abductees have been killed.[7] Colonel Charles Hoge, director of the Division of Psychiatry and Neuroscience at Walter Reed Army Institute of Research, testified before the U.S. House of Representatives Committee on Veterans' Affairs in late September 2006 that approximately 10 to 15 percent of the veterans returning from Iraq screen positive for PTSD, depression, or anxiety twelve months after homecoming.[8] Their stories dominate the news and certainly demand respect and understanding, but a truer account of military experiences would include in the discourse of the study of veterans the examination of adaptation.[9] Less discussed are the lives of the soldiers who return from war resilient and ready to reenter their civilian lives. The narratives of soldiers such as Kate Arnold, Vince Stephenson, and Zach Bendock offer rich insights into alternative deployment experiences. They demonstrate abilities to move from life as primarily a civilian to life as a full-time soldier and back with few negative residual consequences while returning to the States proud of their accomplishments. But a substantial number of their colleagues in the 893rd have stories to tell that are quite different yet also fail to fit neatly into popular representations of wartime soldiering.

five

Struggling Reservists

"Everything Back Home Has Become So Confusing"

And sometimes I was wishin' I was still back in Iraq, 'cause none of my prob-lems were really back there. I didn't have my problems with my ex back there, and I didn't have to worry about it 'cause I was doin' other stuff. But when I got home, I had to worry about it then, and it's just like it was as if it was hard to let go.
— *Enlisted Army Reservist Dennis Harris*

Over the course of his multiple deployments, Dennis Harris, an enlistee barely into his twenties, was trying to juggle the competing demands of being a reservist, a civilian security guard, a son, a brother, a boyfriend turned fiancé, a potential stepfather to his fiancée's two young children, an ex-fiancé, and father to a newborn infant son. In reflecting on his life since 9/11, Dennis sees his day-to-day, homegrown civilian problems as more onerous to navigate than serving as a soldier in a makeshift prison in the midst of a war zone. He is not alone in this experience. Just over a third of the reservists we came to know are struggling much as Den-nis is with civilian lives that were troubled before 9/11 and have grown more troubling since. With one exception, all are male reservists.

Homegrown Struggles

In developing the questions to spark our conversations with members of the 893rd, we were keenly aware of the possibility of producing secondary trauma by asking newly returned veterans about their war experiences. We conferred with several war veterans who cautioned us that seemingly innocuous questions could bring about unanticipated responses from war-weary soldiers. General William Tecumseh Sherman famously declared following the American Civil War that "war is hell."[1] We did not intend specifically to elicit stories of hellish events. The 893rd was not involved in direct combat, but the war in Iraq has rarely been depicted as having clear front lines and noncombat zones. While many company members felt relatively safe in their living compound just off the grounds of their prison camp, they were nonetheless routinely subjected to potentially life-threatening events. From the air flight into Baghdad under the cover of darkness to the final convoy south to Kuwait, the dangers in Iraq were realities of everyday life. Those who either volunteered or were assigned to prisoner transfer missions were always at risk of encountering roadside improvised explosive devices (IEDs), mortar attacks on the prison camp were routine, broken-down vehicles left soldiers sitting ducks in the heart of urban centers, and prisoner uprisings, while rare, were always on the soldiers' minds. Add to this mix the culture shock of witnessing absolute poverty among the Iraqi people and deplorable prison conditions, and it seems only natural that reservists should struggle to return to normal civilian life.

When stepping into their reserve center to begin our conversations, we expected to hear many stories of soldiers returning from the trauma of war and struggling to reintegrate into the civilian worlds that had moved on in their absence. The research literature, media representations of war, and news coverage are all heavily skewed toward the experiences of soldiers who unpack from their duffle bags not only their material possessions but the newly acquired emotional, psychological, and/or physical baggage of soldiering. We met several reservists who wrestle daily with the repercussions of their war-zone circumstances; however, we found twice as many soldiers whose stories focus on homegrown struggles that predate 9/11 and are deeply rooted in their civilian biographies. We were completely taken aback by the number of times members of the 893rd referred to their deployment experiences as a relief from home life or as having been "like a vacation" from home life. The struggling male reservists commonly revealed that deployments simplify life by physically removing them from the complexity and burdens of their civilian home lives.

Equating an extended deployment—particularly in war-torn Iraq—to a vacation seems inconceivable at first glance, but the more we listened to their stories, the more we heard much of the same problems articulated by Arlie Hochschild in *Time Bind: When Work Becomes Home and Home Becomes Work*. Hochschild describes the ways in which many working parents have come to find modern corporate life more fulfilling than the demands of home. Rather than taking advantage of family-friendly policies that would enable parents in dual-earner relationships to spend more time with their families, working parents are quite reluctant to reduce their time at the office. Hochschild explains that as corporate America has become more team oriented through the development of "total quality" principles that value the "internal customer," many large employers are offering seminars such as "Dealing with Anger" or "How to Give and Accept Criticism." In contrast to the workplace, Hochschild explains, home life is devoid of seminars such as "Dealing with Your Child's Disappointment in You" or "How to Treat Your Spouse Like an Internal Customer."[2]

In similar fashion, many of the soldiers that we met talk fondly of the structure, clarity, accountability, responsibility, and teamwork that go hand in hand with working full time on a military mission. Even though they were initially thrown into garrison work at Ft. McHenry that required much on-the-job training, and great confusion—known to some reservists as "cluster fuck"—occurred at the outset of their mission in Iraq, after they settled into both deployments, relative stability was achieved. Individual soldiers soon learned who could be counted on, who to turn to for help, and who was responsible for the tasks at hand. While the military offers manuals that spell out everything from hygiene to court-martial procedures, home life rarely affords any such complete clarity regarding day-to-day operations. Chain of command at home can be muddled, and "standard operating procedures" are left to wide interpretation by each member of a household. For many working-class reservists, their jobs as military police officers—whether garrison work on an American base or guarding prisoners in Iraq—are often more challenging or exciting than their civilian work options. Having the responsibility, for example, of guarding a hundred or more prisoners—some of them among the most notorious members of the original U.S. most-wanted list in Iraq—holds more prestige than many of these struggling reservists' civilian jobs or in some cases the unemployment or layoff that awaits their homecoming.

The struggling reservists we met would certainly benefit from additional military debriefings, meetings with military chaplains, additional discussions with fellow soldiers, and in some cases formal therapy. However, in most cases what they need to discuss even more than warzone-induced struggles are the troubles born of the stresses and strains of their multifaceted civilian worlds, filled with unsteady relationships and shaky jobs. Rather than speak of war-grown demons, nearly three-quarters of the struggling reservists expressed some combination of discontent, disappointment, disillusionment, and disapproval about the circumstances of their civilian lives.[3] For struggling soldiers, troubles come in small and big doses, but they are strung together in their accounts and have strong homegrown roots. When he starts to relay the multitude of civilian problems experienced before and during his deployments, Dennis Harris's comments about wishing to be back in Baghdad seem less irrational. Dennis has the habit of ending many of his statements with either "whatnot" or "you know" and invokes a slightly crooked smile a lot as he continuously laughs at himself and the homegrown obstacles he has encountered. Instead of coming home from Ft. McHenry to a warm and stable home, as adaptive reservists did, Dennis was completely taken aback to find that his father had converted his bedroom into a home office and had moved Dennis's belongings into a rented storage unit. Dennis can laugh about the situation now, but as he tells this story, his sense of disillusionment lies not far below the surface.

I was like, "Well, now I guess I have to move out now." Well, actually, my father, at first when I told [him] I was movin' out, he was like, "You don't have to move out." I'm like, "*Well, where am I gonna sleep?*" He was like, "Well, I thought you were gonna be gone for two years." "Well, I'm not." . . . I then ended up sleeping in my brother's room on his floor for a little while until I found an apartment.

The disappointment in returning to the reality of feeling pushed out of his childhood home turned out to be nothing compared to the devastation caused to Dennis by the woman he loved. Sadly, his life took on a soap-opera-like tone as he relayed the story of their on-again, off-again relationship. After hearing the news that the company was shipping off to Iraq, Dennis hastily asked his girlfriend to marry him. Their engagement was short-lived and complicated by an unplanned pregnancy. Dennis returned home from Iraq in time to witness the birth of his son but wanted little to do with his ex-fiancée, who had reconnected with a former lover and broke Dennis's heart as he sat in the Iraqi desert. By the time we spoke with Dennis, just a few months after the birth of his son, his ex-fiancée and her current lover had absconded with the infant to another region of the states, leaving Dennis with no knowledge of their whereabouts.

The group of struggling reservists includes not only Dennis but nearly all of the other men who got engaged or sped-up wedding plans in conjunction with the news of one of their deployments.[4] Many newlyweds married just prior to 9/11 who had limited time to establish their marriages are also prominent among the struggling reservists. With the institutional transformation of the part-time reservists into full-time soldiers, these girlfriends, fiancées, or newlywed wives often initiate "Dear John" letters and phone calls that play out close to the popular representation of wartime soldiering. In contrast, nearly all of the soldiers who were married for at least seven years are among the adaptive reservists. Whether married or single, the adaptive soldiers could consistently count on solid civilian networks to support their expansive soldiering role, whereas struggling reservists—whether newly married, engaged, or single—went into their deployments with thin, unstable, and troubled civilian networks and came home to them as well. It is

hard to convey the sadness in Michelle Colton's voice when she juxtaposes the imaginary homecoming scenario she held onto in Iraq with
the reality of the disappointment she faced:

> I imagined coming, all family and friends and they are all cheering,
> signs, and, you know, they would have the band and stuff there. And
> I imagined they're being in formation and saying, "Dismissed," and
> you know, you run up to your family and you get all these cool hugs
> and stuff. And I couldn't wait to see my friend—even [though] she
> never wrote me, I still wanted to see her and get to see my goddaugh-
> ter and things like that, and go home and have a nice dinner—some-
> thing. That was what I imagined it to be, and what happened was
> completely different.
>
> Nobody was there. I had nobody. My mom had just had a surgery,
> so she couldn't make it. The weather was bad, so some people didn't
> want to chance driving in the snow. My friend never returned any
> calls, so she never showed up, and I'm, like, "Okay." So I came home,
> and they said, "Dismissed," and the only person I had to go to was
> one of the guys in our unit that was sent home early. He's like my
> brother, so I gave him a hug. But that was it, and I'm walking around.
> He gave me his cell phone. . . . I only got a hold of my mom, and I
> wanted to call my friend, and I dialed the wrong number, and it's early
> in the morning—it's, like, 7:30 in the morning. I woke this person up
> out of bed and I was, "Hello?" [And she said,] "Honey, I think you
> have the wrong number." And I said, "I'm sorry. I didn't mean to
> wake you up. I just got back from Baghdad." And this person that I
> didn't even know starts thanking me, and I'm just like, "Lady, you
> have no idea. You have just made me feel so much better," because
> I'm, like, all sad because there was nobody there.
>
> Then this [colonel] came up to me, and I was like, "Okay, I'm sup-
> posed to be at attention or something for you," and he's like, "Hey, do
> you have any family here?" And I said, "No." He's like, "Can I give
> you a hug?" I'm like, "Sure." He gives me a hug, and he says, "You've
> just been hugged by the chaplain. You know you have been blessed."

Unlike their more adaptive colleagues, who often had prior active-
duty deployment experience to draw upon, only one of the struggling sol-

diers had any experience with a full deployment prior to 9/11. The men and one woman we call struggling soldiers embrace their newly expanded role as full-time soldiers, but their loved ones are unprepared for what the country will demand in the months and years following the 9/11 attacks. Prior to the deployments, Dennis Harris lived with his father and his slightly younger brother. As the older brother, Dennis looked after his sibling, but in the context of the deployments his younger brother had a difficult time stepping up his level of responsibility.

> It affected my brother 'cause before I left, I used to have to wake him up to go to school. I'd drive him to school sometimes 'cause he was always gettin' up late. And when I left, he missed a lot of school days and whatnot. I've always been watchin' after him. . . . My brother was kinda—he was stressed out 'cause he got thrown in [to responsibility], he had power of attorney over me. He had to pay all the bills. He was really stressed out at that point 'cause he had to deal with everything.

Not only was Dennis's brother stressed out by the deployments, but his girlfriend/fiancée/ex-fiancée, who completely opposed Dennis's decision to join the reserves, became distraught during the deployments and had to be medicated to help alleviate her anxiety.

The standard drill of one weekend a month and two weeks a year is a time commitment away from civilian social networks but amounted to nothing in comparison to the extended deployments, even if the first one was on the safety of U.S. soil. As their military roles expand, full-time soldiering responsibilities add to what are already stressed civilian lives. Deployments do not erase family civilian stresses but instead either amplify or postpone conflicts. Jorge Mercado, an officer who married between the two deployments, taps the conference room table nervously as he explains,

> A great deal has changed personally, only because of the family and because of on top of the marriage that I haven't really participated in for a whole year. And so everything has really been delayed. All the little squabbles and things that you encounter in the first few years of marriage, it's starting to catch up with me now, so—put the toilet seat

down and stuff like that. Yeah, those kind of things are just now surfacing, and now I have to balance those things with this new responsibility and going back to work, so it's hard. And it changed me in a sense that I still want to serve my country, and I still want to do the right thing, and I just need to find a more family-friendly way of doing it. So that's where I'm sitting right now.

During our conversation, Jorge generally offers long answers to questions, and in the midst of his stories, he sometimes loses his train of thought, asking, "Where was I?" However, as he draws on a particularly strong cinematic image that he uses for guidance, he has no difficulty staying focused. In explaining his efforts to meet the competing demands in his life, his voice contains more than a hint of pain:

Did you ever see *We Were Soldiers,* with Mel Gibson? . . . There's one scene in particular where this young lieutenant comes up to Mel Gibson—he's the colonel. Mel Gibson is this family man, wife and five kids, and he's career military. And the new lieutenant comes up to him, he's in church, and they're both praying, and he says, "Sir," he says, "do you think—do you find that doing this job and raising a family, does it help you or does it hinder you?" And Mel Gibson just stops for a second and he goes, "Well," he goes, "I just hope that," he says, "I just hope that being good at one makes me better at the other." And that just that's how I try to approach it.

Finding a family-friendly way to be plucked from the everyday civilian world and the network of people for whom a soldier has reciprocal responsibilities requires adjustments on both sides, a quality not stressed within the Gibson film and an attribute missing for many of the struggling soldiers. The struggling soldiers either pick up and carry their civilian stresses into deployments as heavy baggage or embrace their deployments as an escape route from their stateside circumstances. Almost all of them became deeply committed to their positions and responsibilities within the military. Many came home from Ft. McHenry or Iraq wanting to transfer to the active-duty army but were unable to do so because of the entanglements of their personal lives. All of them found it impossible to strike a balance between military desires and expectations and home life responsibilities and expectations. They struggle with the repercussions of having willingly embraced their fuller commitment to the military or wanting desperately to move to the active-duty side of the military while being tethered to civilian life by family members unwilling or unable to make that institutional leap with them.

Circumstances of Homegrown Struggles

At the outset of his classic novel, *Anna Karenina,* Leo Tolstoy notes, "Happy families are all alike; every unhappy family is unhappy in its own way."[5] The struggling soldiers of the 893rd provide narratives of homegrown discontent that are as unique as they are convergent with one another. What defines their coherence as struggling reservists is that they depict a downward spiral in the social circumstances of their home lives, reveal unrealistic expectations of people in their civilian lives that go unmet, employ strategies of avoidance to cope with their growing frustrations, and wrap themselves in the language and relationships of wartime brotherhood. These men and one woman, Michelle Colton, narrate more than one of these elements of discontent, setting them apart from the 893rd's adaptive and resistant reservists.

Civilian Life Happens

A consequence of the advent of the all-volunteer army is the fact that the demographics of the military have shifted away from primarily young, unmarried male soldiers to a greater proportion of older soldiers, female soldiers, married soldiers, soldiers with children, and soldiers married to other soldiers.[6] In conjunction with these demographic shifts, observers have called for an emphasis on developing family-friendly policies for married soldiers.[7] While every effort should be made to alleviate the strains of soldiering on spouses and children, as Michelle Colton's story illustrates, civilian lives of single soldiers can also involve significant family responsibilities. Young soldiers living on the edge of the economy and without substantial education often tell stories of complex civilian lives that are overwhelming even before the army has pulled the soldiers several thousand miles away. For these reservists, deployments further fray lives already heavily worn down by civilian circumstances.

❖ Trevor Scott

With a strong note of exasperation that echoes Dennis Harris's yearnings to escape the complexities of civilian life for the simplicity of deployment life, Trevor Scott, a young stocky enlistee, exclaims,

> The deployments themselves have been fun. It's just coming home that's been really bad. It's not fun. Just everything back home has become so confusing, it's just a relief to just get away from it and concentrate on whatever the army wants us to do.

Everything back home in his rural community was continuing to unravel for Trevor. While Trevor found he could rely on several key close military colleagues for almost anything, his family life at home was full of troubles that his deployments only exacerbated.

> In June my father got sick and was put in the hospital. They told us they weren't expecting him to make it until more than a day. So the unit flew me home for that. He pulled through that, but he had to be put in a nursing home. So I was there for about a week, then came home and came back to Ft. McHenry. And then in August he passed away in the nursing home, and I flew back for four days, then back to Ft. McHenry. . . .
> And somewhere in the midst of all that, my fiancée and I broke up. It was a really, really bad year down there. Within a six-month period, my brother was diagnosed with a cancerous tumor in his kidney, and that had to be removed. Then he got himself in a bunch of trouble and ended up getting arrested for writing bad checks and went to jail. My father had gotten sick and passed away. My sister had a fire in one of the bedrooms in the house that pretty much between the smoke and all that pretty much destroyed the downstairs of the house. So they were staying with my mother. Three days after her house, the alternator on her car caught fire. My fiancée and I broke up. And I laid my

motorcycle down. I think that was everything. It was a long six-month period that nothing would go right.

With the exception of the breakup with his fiancée, which he attributes to her unwillingness to stick through a long-distance relationship, the problems that arise for Trevor's family are not deployment related. Amid the backdrop of the rapid changes in his family life, Trevor found coming home from Ft. McHenry quite disconcerting:

> [It was] really different. My father passed away in August. Up until that point, I had never been at my house pretty much by myself. My dad retired, took an early retirement, so there was always someone there at the house. We always—our family got together every holiday. I went home—it was just my mom and I, with one of my sisters and one of my brothers stopping by once in a while. My mom got remarried and moved out, and I took over the running the house that we'd lived in. I went from always being around my parents to living in the barracks with three hundred soldiers to living by myself. It was just kinda weird. So I slept there, worked a lot, and just hung out at the fire station any time I was awake. I was hardly ever at my house.

Because he did not approve of her remarriage, Trevor's relationship with his mother deteriorated markedly between deployments. Rather than further straining their relationship, however, the second deployment helped to mend the rift with his mother: "I don't know if we would have started speaking again if I hadn't been deployed. The second deployment has brought us somewhat back together," he recalls.

Trevor was "relieved" to hear that the 893rd was shipping to Iraq, noting, "Everything was so much different at home that [deploying again] was getting back into somethin' familiar." Although his relationship with his mother was improving, she still let him down in terms of support, and he chuckles slightly as he recalls his request for a care package:

> At one point, I had asked her to send me a package, and I gave her a list of stuff, and she was supposed to pay for it out of my checking account and all that. And *she gave me the stuff when I got home.*

If his family life was unraveling while he was stateside at Ft. McHenry, the situation only worsened while Trevor was in Iraq.

> While I was gone, I let one of my brothers stay with me—the one that had gotten out of jail and he needed a place to stay, and so he was staying with me. My mom was taking care of all my bills for me for the house. He told her, "I'm paying this one, this one, this one, and this one." And she ended up throwing him out because the police were at my house apparently four weeks in a row. So she ended up throwing him out of the house, and then she started getting cancellation notices for a bunch of utilities. Apparently he hadn't paid anything. So all the money I made in Iraq went to paying back utility bills for the house, and I made a little bit less during the three months at the mobilization site, and I started getting a little bit behind on bills there. Then we got deployed, the combat pay was enough to pay 'em. But because he had let them get so far behind, all the money I made in Iraq went there. So I came home from seven months in Iraq with about $350 to show for it. And as a result, now I'm living in an apartment in a friend's basement because I couldn't afford the house anymore. I just sold my Jeep Cherokee because I'm still trying to pay back some of the bills from the house still. I'm just trying to play catch-up financially.

Trevor Scott never brings home the strain of war, and in fact, his friends are prone to remark on how little they feel he has changed over course of the deployments. In his absence, his home life has become confusing, and deployments represent an environment of less discontent. But while Trevor's financial problems grew over the course of his deployments, Lee Gauthier's civilian dreams were unraveling well before he ever stepped into his first deployment.

❖ Lee Gauthier

When Lee Gauthier came into the conference room to begin his interview, he slumped quietly in his chair with his shoulders hunched over and his chin drooped toward his chest. Lee's despondent demeanor was unlike the body language of many of the soldiers we interviewed during the 893rd's drill weekends. The reservists generally began their interviews seated in a relatively rigid posture, looking at us directly as they spoke and defensively waiting for the questions that lay ahead. Within a few minutes of talking with us, the defenses usually came down, the postures relaxed, and the discussions tended to become much more animated. Most of the struggling reservists told their stories with at least a hint of humor or irony intertwined, but Lee rarely smiled as he mumbled about his difficulties in seeing his way through his civilian problems. Talking with Lee and learning that he is a returning veteran of the war in Iraq, combined with his overall state of depression, might lead to the assumption that he is suffering from PTSD, but the sources of Lee's troubles are almost completely homegrown, and he now wants to go active duty for what he hopes would be a stateside post. Although Lee talks very briefly about having seen dead bodies in Iraq, he is much more preoccupied with the events of his home life that have completely derailed his dreams and aspirations of playing college football and pursuing a career in law enforcement. Lee complains that he is now out of shape, with the muscle tone more indicative of a manual laborer—primarily upper-body strength—than the overall sculpted physique of a well-trained athlete.

Lee joined the Reserve as a junior in high school, a full year before the 9/11 attacks. As captain of his high school football team, Lee's prospects for playing NCAA Division III college football were promising, although he is relatively short; however, he had not planned on becoming a father during his senior year after a pregnancy resulted from a one-night stand.

> Before I left for Iraq, I had a son, so that kinda messed me up because that's like I wasn't in a relationship with the girl or nothin', and before I left for Iraq, I found out she was pregnant, and it just wasn't the greatest thing in my life. Messed a lot with it. . . . I get [the baby] every other weekend and on Wednesdays, but it's pretty hard for me. It's like I don't want to have nothing to do with it.

Lee's struggles stem from his feeling pushed into the responsibility for a child he did not want. To compound matters, Lee feels that his college football dream has been shattered not only because of the weight of fatherhood but also because he has missed out on strenuous physical training during his time in Iraq. When he couples being out of shape with the financial responsibility for an infant, college and football now lie well beyond his reach. To make matters worse, a minor altercation with the law cost Lee his dream of becoming a police officer.

Lee is one of several soldiers who complain about not being able to sleep since returning from Iraq, but he seems to attribute this symptom more to his derailed civilian life than anything deployment related. In just over a year's worth of time, Lee went from being the captain of his high school football team with bright prospects to a marginalized young man working a manual labor job he despises to pay for the needs of child he never intended to father. When he steps back to assess his life, he seems overwhelmed by the weight of his homegrown responsibilities:

> It's pretty stressful. I just think I don't have enough time in life anymore. I have no time, and I'm young. It kinda kills me responsibility-wise. I don't know. I just wish I could do everything, but I get held back because of my parents and stuff. It's kinda hard for me. I can't do what I want all the time. You know, I gotta be there for—it's like if I want to go out and do something, I have to, like, take my kid that day. . . . I just wasn't ready for it, and [my parents] were making me, trying to get ready for it, and it doesn't help. I'd like to have gotten into [it] on my own time when I had like, you know—I like moving into it on my own time, but they're pushing me into it, but—I don't know. I don't like it. Everybody's like, "You have a kid now. You got to take care of it." I know I have to take care of it. I pay for it every week. And "You've got to see it here, you've got to see it there, and you've got to do all this," and it's like—I don't know. I'm not ready for it. I'm just not. I'm responsible, but I'm not like a strict, strict kind of responsibility. I know my limits and everything, but I just ain't up there yet for that.

All of the reservists we spoke with were living complex civilian lives prior to 9/11. They did the same things in which so many people are involved on a day-to-day civilian basis, including going to school or work, caring for family members, juggling civilian jobs while serving their part-time military duties, and engaging in the million little details of life, like making car payments. Struggling reservists such as Trevor Scott and Lee Gauthier reveal little in the way of social tools to manage their complexity and lack the support networks to help them bring order to their lives.

When "Support the Troops" Does Not Start at Home

When we conducted our interviews with members of the 893rd, outright symbols of patriotic support of the troops in Iraq and Afghanistan such as storefront signs and yellow magnetic car ribbons were pervasive. The reservists spoke nostalgically about the letters, e-mails, and care packages they received from folks back home. We heard many stories of new friendships forged through the kindness of people who, not more that casual acquaintances prior to the war, went to great lengths to support the reservists while they were stationed in Iraq. Care packages carry great practical and sentimental value to the reservists. The members of the 893rd lived in a compound next to the prison, lacking many of the amenities that became available as the army built larger, more permanent bases later in the war. The small military-run convenience store, referred to as a PX, had relatively few items, particularly at the outset of the war. In one particularly witty moment, Barry Watts explains the value of something as simple as powdered drink mixes to soldiers stationed in the desert:

> KoolAid was like crack—I mean, you can go in the corner and like sell back the KoolAid, and I'm serious you would make a lot of money. Juice, Hi-C, stuff like that, I mean—I could make a lot of money out there with just Gatorade, you know, sell those little baggies. Yeah, 'cause drinking the plain water got old after a while—you needed something.

Amid the stories of remarkable support, however, are also stories of both unmet and unrealistic expectations about loved ones' inability to provide the support the reservists expect during their time away. These stories are sometimes expressed with anger or guilt just underneath the surface as struggling reservists describe disappointments with wives or girlfriends. Some reveal stories of resentment toward wives who soldiers felt were less than receptive to phone calls placed in the middle of the night, while others express guilt about the emotional state of a wife, girlfriend, or fiancée. While many adaptive male reservists narrate stories of how deployment experiences strengthen long-term marriages, the same did not hold true for many newly formed romantic attachments or young marriages that frayed or snapped under the strain of the multiple deployments. For some of these women, keeping up with the demands of a civilian life now devoid of the reservists' presence was an overwhelming enough experience without having to add to household, employment, educational, and/or parenting duties the emotional support sought by their deployed partners.[8] Having pushed for marriage, engagement, or living together just ahead of and between deployments, these troubled reservists have unrealistic expectations that the women in their lives will reorient themselves as dedicated, civilian partners of deployed soldiers. Luke Fisher, the self-described selfish person discussed earlier, tells of his disappointment.

❖ Luke Fisher

Luke Fisher's disappointment in and resentment toward his wife develop and fester while he is in Iraq and cut straight to the heart of his postdeployment marital troubles. He seems unable to forgive or forget his wife's failure to send letters or care packages as often as he wished. He is not really in a joking mood when he states,

> Me and my driver, he's one of my team members, we would joke about chartering a jet, getting one of the fighter pilots to come home and drop a bomb because we haven't received any letters. We needed to get them to drop a bomb because we have not gotten a letter in a while. But it was the mail system, they were the—well, that's what I'm told. The letters were held up by the [postal system]. Yeah, it's in the mail—you know, check's in the mail. . . . I have no idea why. I've heard the excuses, but I don't believe them, but I don't know. I have no idea.

The mail system seemed to work just fine for everyone else who was sending items to Luke, so he thinks that skepticism is warranted:

> I had other friends send the letters, so—I mean, we depended on each other a lot. I mean, not really financially because there was nothing to buy there, you know. We didn't—there was a PX there, but it didn't have much, and we just counted on family members to send us what we needed or wanted. And when [my friend's] family members sent him something that I liked or he knew I liked or I might want, he was like, "So, why don't you take this?"—you know, such and such— "She sent this," or "Take this," you know. And I'm a KoolAid drinker, I love KoolAid, and I made a bet with somebody that I would not drink any soda while I was there, so I had everybody sending KoolAid—everybody's mom was sending me KoolAid.

Luke seems unable to recognize the work his wife had put into their home, her continuing education, and the full-time responsibility of raising their toddler son; instead, he focuses on having endured the hardships of war without tangible evidence of support. This building resentment toward his wife left Luke uncertain about wanting to come home.

> I didn't look forward to it. I didn't. I was upset. Because I didn't get the response or the support that I guess—the support I thought I should have had. I anticipated a lot, but it wasn't that way. . . . So when I didn't receive that, when it was actually time to come home, I didn't expect homecoming to be good at all. It was better than I thought. I guess even though I didn't get the support, she—I mean, when I saw her again for the first time after—what—nine months, I missed her a lot. I realized that. I didn't think I missed her when I was there, but I missed my son. Boy, that boy grew a lot. So it was good.

Although Luke warmed initially to his wife after seeing her, he was less happy about transitioning out of full-time army life. Were it not for his responsibilities to his wife and child, he would definitely transition to active duty and volunteer for more missions. Instead, he says, transitioning back to civilian life as been "forced upon me."

It's a bit disappointing, because I like army life. I like the fact that everything is—it's set. You know you have to do something at this time, and it follows a schedule. But being home, there is no schedule, you know—I mean, there's a schedule: You know, you wake up, you go to work, [my son] goes to school, you come home. But it's not the same as army life. Like I can eat whenever I want to here. I guess I could have eaten whenever I wanted to there, but in the army there are guidelines that you follow. You have to do certain things at a certain time. Here it's not, and it's like, man, I miss it. I miss the army. I want to go back, but I have other responsibilities, and the army doesn't pay enough.

Like his colleagues, Luke was warned in the debriefing sessions held in Kuwait that returning home would be difficult because spouses tend to develop their own routines during deployments and can be reluctant to relinquish power to the returnees; however, Luke's wife had no problem calling on Luke actively to parent their son.

My wife had our son for the last two years, so I guess she figures she needs a break—and rightfully so. I mean, she has been raising the child as a single parent for two years now. So she does her thing. I'm going to say does her thing—it's not like she just leaves, but Tuesdays, Wednesdays, and Thursdays, our son is with me, and this started [right after we got back], so Tuesdays, Wednesdays, Thursdays, and Saturdays. And it's like, hey? He was in preschool, and he got homework. I don't know why. You're not supposed to get preschool homework. But he got homework, so I had to help him do his homework, and I'm like, "God, I hate this." I'm serious. So it was a—I don't know. The full-time responsibility was disappointing, very much so, but you know, that's the life I chose, I guess, so I had to take care of those responsibilities.

Despite feeling disappointed in life since his return home, Luke has grown extremely close to his son, and as he talks about how his deployment has changed him, Luke focuses on the tight relationship he has developed with his son to the exclusion of his wife.

I'm a lot more selfish. Yes, very much so. I was selfish before, but now I mean it's like it's just me and my son. That's it. I don't care about anything else. That's it. She does her thing. I don't know—she goes out every once in a while, you know. We have family time—well, me and my son have family time. Tuesday nights are family nights. We will go out and eat at a different restaurant every Tuesday night. Usually it spills over to Wednesday nights you know, 'cause there's someplace else or if I don't feel like cooking. So every once in a while she'll go with us, but [usually] it's just me and my son.

When asked where his wife is on a "family night" that involves just him and his son, Luke explains coldly,

I don't invite her. I mean, most of the time—I mean, Tuesday nights is family nights, but a lot of times it's spur-of-the-moment. . . . Go visit Pop Pop, or we'll go visit so and so, or we'll go out and play in the park or something. But you know she'll find out when we are going out the door that night. . . . So she's not really invited.

Luke's iciness toward his wife started while he was situated in the oppressive heat of the desert; however, the bigger problem they face as he transitions back from the military is his desire not to leave full-time soldiering. The majority of the struggling reservists want to remain in the military, and this desire serves as a wedge in their civilian relationships.

Choosing Army Green

For many struggling reservists, the deployment orders served as an escape route from overwhelming or undesirable home circumstances. This strategy, crafted consciously or not, only further damages civilian relationships frayed prior to the deployments.

Ed Mertz is an enthusiastic soldier who thrives on the responsibility that comes with his high-ranking NCO status. Ed is completely at home in his BDUs and talks, more than any of his colleagues, of how much he feels that all soldiers, whether in his own company or not, are part of what he considers his extended family. With friends in high places, Ed reports having plenty of warning that should the United States invade Iraq, the 893rd would likely be deployed. When he returned from the Ft. McHenry deployment, Ed's fiancée strongly encouraged him to take the opportunity to retire from the reserves, but Ed insisted he could not send the company to Iraq in his absence. When he chose the military over his civilian ties, his fiancée—now ex-fiancée—called him a "warmonger." In his defense, Ed explains,

> I could've stayed in the States. But that's not me. I've looked at this company as my family, my kids. . . . We had that special bond—you know, that special trust that was usually hard. . . . And it's basically my job to bring 'em back alive . . . either for Ft. McHenry or for Iraq. It's my job to bring these guys back in one piece. And it's my job to keep 'em that way, and the only thing I can't account for is their stupidity—I mean, not paying attention doin' something, something we've trained them.

Likewise, Derek Henry could have stayed home from Iraq because of a medical condition. A seasoned, senior NCO, Derek was one of the few company members deployed as a reservist during the 1991 Gulf War, so he knows what wartime reserve deployment looks and feels like. Although Derek speaks affectionately about the soldiers under his command, he has the demeanor of a high-ranking sergeant who could certainly strike the fear of God into new recruits. Derek is relatively nonchalant about how the deployments affected him as an individual, but he admits that deploying to Iraq was especially difficult for his teenage children, who resent Derek both for purposely placing himself in danger and for exhibiting a stronger allegiance to the military than to his family. Both Ed and Derek, with their long-standing commitments to the military and their status as NCOs, turn away from their family circumstances and immerse themselves in soldiering, satisfied to work on repairing civilian damage when they get home. If Ed and Derek are conscious of their decision to choose army green over their civilian ties, other reservists, such as Chad Holmes, are less conscious of their deployment actions and the repercussions of pushing family away during their deployments.

❖ Chad Holmes

Just prior to 9/11, Chad Holmes had transferred from ten years of state-side active-duty experience to the reserve system in hopes of pursing a civilian career in law enforcement. When we spoke with him, he had just recently been reassigned to the 893rd to fill one of several top positions left vacant by the rapid postdeployment reassignments and retirements. When asked to describe himself, Chad gives a big smile: "Well, I'm goofy. I like the army." He is exceedingly enthusiastic and can barely wait for us to ask a question before jumping in with a helpful answer. He is proud of the fact that despite having initially married his wife, Amy, because of an unplanned pregnancy, through counseling they have grown to love and cherish each other. Their love is apparent as his freckled face softens each time he speaks of her or their daughter. Chad explains with some degree of pain the couple's difficulties in their relatively young marriage and attributes these problems to his behavior in Iraq and his subsequent return home. While stationed in Iraq, Chad's company had been assigned a dangerous mission with limited equipment to carry out their duties, and Chad turned his focus exclusively to the tasks at hand. He apologetically states,

> I was a terrible husband. I got mail from her—well, the first two or three months, we didn't get any mail, then we started getting it, and I'd get a letter from her like at least every two weeks. But I was terrible. The whole environment just scared the shit out of me. I thought every day I was going to die, and that goes to the people I served with in the training and stuff like that. We had no equipment, and I was scared shitless. The only thing I could think about was keeping myself alive and my soldiers. So, actually I got so scared one night we got hit so hard, I started keeping a journal and I told them in there that if I died, you know, I wanted them to know what was going on over there and stuff like that—how much I loved them and cared about 'em. But as far as expressing it in letters or calling 'em, we didn't have access to phone until like two weeks before I left country. We were like out in the boonies. So I didn't—I was terrible, you know.
>
> Now that I get home and we've talked about it, I felt bad because that hurt her because she had no idea, you know, how I was. If I was

hurt, if I was getting mail and stuff. And she talked to a couple of my buddies like my platoon sergeant. He and I are like best friends, and she talked to his wife and he'd be like sending her flowers from somewhere and letters all the time. That really hurt her, which now I see the importance of it, and as a leader I want to make sure my soldiers at least write a letter and say hi to their family. It's important. But, yeah, I was terrible. All I thought about was my soldiers that were there, and they all had issues. They'd come to me about problems going on back home, and they were scared and stuff, so that was my whole world. That was my family. I kinda blocked everybody out that year in Iraq, and I think that hurt us a lot when I got home.

Amy's lack of support from Chad during the deployment is compounded by the fact that she has a limited civilian support system. Chad describes Amy as an introvert who is not comfortable socializing and trying to make new friends. With her isolation exacerbated by her parents' relocation to a different state during the Iraq deployment, Amy was miserable during his deployment and is having a hard time learning to trust him again. As he reflects back on his deployment time and the way in which he shut his wife out of his life in Iraq, Chad is quite candid in his characterizing his own shortcomings as a husband and father:

I thought that because she was always doing nice stuff for me and everything that she deserved better, you know—find a guy that would treat her the way she treats me. I was in that environment where I couldn't take care of 'em, see 'em, you know, touch 'em, hold 'em. So, for me, that was hard. My soldiers became my family. Making sure they were safe, staying on them, doing stuff like that.

Add to the Mix War-Grown Struggles

Wartime deployment struggles, as these stories show, commonly arise from civilian circumstances. In some cases, however, this mixture incorporates the problems that can arise, as Chad Holmes illustrates, from the circumstances of a war zone. Chad is among a small grouping of struggling reservists who recount stories that combine homegrown and war-grown problems. It is impossible to disentangle whether the emotional problems they describe—excessive anger or aggression, depression, and lack of tolerance in particular—stem from their frayed civilian lives or the war zone. Like other struggling reservists, they have troubled civilian lives, but they also narrate ways that serving in a war zone changes aspects of their personalities that poorly fit civilian expectations. Lionel Johnson has homegrown struggles that include a wife who could not provide the level of support he desired, his having chosen to go to Iraq despite having been eligible for a family hardship exemption, and his crushed dreams of becoming a career military man. These unmet expectations, avoidance strategies, and civilian circumstances are intertwined with the war-zone baggage he tries to unpack after returning home.

❖ Lionel Johnson

Like Lee Gauthier, Lionel sits through our conversation as if he has never learned the military's personal-carriage directives. Lionel has a difficult time maintaining eye contact, opting instead to stare vacantly at the conference room table. He is a relatively slender man of average height, and the fact that he cannot seem to project his voice above a barely audible mumble makes him seem even smaller in stature. His tightly cut black hair does not move as he tilts his head to the side with quiet resignation. Lionel joined the reserves in his early twenties, looking for a way to finance some college courses. He came out of basic training and was assigned to a sister MP company of the 893rd. Just as he was starting to put the wheels in motion to begin college, his former company, like the 893rd, was deployed for a year's worth of garrison duty to a different stateside military base, Ft. Kinley. With limited family responsibilities at the time, Lionel not only took this deployment in stride but came to appreciate the ways in which the military helped to mature him and provides him with a network of close colleagues who pull together to help one and other. Given the strong sense of camaraderie and positive changes to his life that he gained at Ft. Kinley, Lionel laments the loss of his military career in the face of new civilian family responsibilities:

I missed the army. I missed the active duty real bad. A couple of days, just waking up, I just wanted to call the recruiter and say, "I want to go active duty." But I knew I had a child on the way with my girlfriend at the time, and I couldn't take that chance of jumping around the country and not being here for my daughter.

Like several other members of the 893rd, Lionel got married shortly after returning home from the garrison duty deployment and began to establish his life with his new wife and her toddler daughter. In addition, Lionel stays connected to his previous girlfriend and their new-born baby.

If Lionel missed army life, he was certain to gain an even bigger dose of it in the coming months as he was involuntarily transferred to the 893rd just prior to the Iraq deployment. Although he was eligible to defer his deployment because of complications with his daughter's birth, Lionel decided to deploy to Iraq with the unit. When he speaks of this deployment and its negative impact on his life, we start to understand more about the defeated demeanor he projects:

After this last deployment, it's changed me in a negative way, because it's made me more aggressive and a lot less patient, more confrontational, and a lot—I'm very picky and anal, that's pretty much. . . . For nine months, you can't let anything slide. So now all of a sudden, you get home, you're supposed to—it's just hard to turn it off. . . . When you are dealing with grown men [as prisoners], I think it is just natural, just human nature, where you have to make your stand. You have to display your dominance in order to keep control over situations. We have one guard to one-hundred-plus grown men. You have to always come across as "I'm the main guy," and in order to do that you have to stay on top of them. Every time something happens, you have to be there to catch it. You have to make sure there's nothing going on. You have to always be on top, so, and that affects you once you get home because once you live like that, it's hard to turn it off. . . .

It's been really hard. It's been really hard. I can't be around a lot of people. When I first got home, I couldn't eat out around a lot of people. It just made me feel paranoid. I felt real edgy around a lot of people. Even at work, like if I'm in a closed-in area, I can't have people sitting behind me where I can't see everybody. That's just it, and I don't like being this way, so it's an adjustment.

It is really killing my marriage right now, because she can't understand why I'm acting the way I'm acting. She don't like seeing me the way that I am, you know. Because she knows that I don't like being this way. And I was an aggressive person in one point of my life, and I said I wouldn't really be like that again, so now it's just something that you don't want to be, and it's like you can't control it, so that's it. We tried marriage counseling, but the marriage counselor can't help something that's within me. It can only help us as a married couple, so I don't know. I guess I will try and find something, working to just focus on me.

Lionel attributes the return of aggression to his personality from having been situated in a severely understaffed prison, but the depression he projects and the internal turmoil he experiences also stem from an internal tug-of-war between his personal desire to be a full-time soldier—even after the Iraq deployment and subsequent personality disruption—and his inability to pursue this goal for fear of the toll it will take on his children. Lionel's difficulties with his wife are also intertwined with his disappointment in what he feels was her low level of support during his deployments.

Just simple things, like not sending me a care package, like once a month or every three weeks. Just so—you know, it doesn't feel so good when everybody else is getting packages, and you know, "Where's my freakin' package?" Just stuff like that, just small things, just to let you know that, you know, I really took some time out of my day to send you something. A letter is fine. You can take a day to write a letter, but when you take the time out of your day to actually send a care package, I mean, that took some time because you have to go to the store, go to the post office, and mail it off. So [I wish she could have] just been a little more supportive. But once I got home, she told me that she was going through a really big depression while I was gone. So I try to be understanding of that. It's hard, but I'm trying. Just like I'm going through something by being home now, I have to understand that she went through something while I was gone.

Lionel finds little comfort in his civilian life, and to compensate he longs for the security he felt working toward a common goal alongside his military colleagues. Having grown accustomed to the ways in which the military cared for him as a full-time soldier, Lionel ends his interview with us by expressing his disappointment in the disconnect he feels between what he would like the military to continue to provide and what is actually available to him.

> I just want my country to take care of me. When I come home from deployment, I mean, all that action stuff—I don't need more. I don't want more money, and nothing like that. It's just whenever you send some soldiers—whenever soldiers get sent to combat or a hostile environment, have something there to take care of them. Don't just treat them like whatever when they get home, 'cause that's what we do—we get treated like whatever. So when you first get home, they have a big whoop-de-doo about your being home. A few weeks later, a few months later, you're nothing. That's not right. It's not.

❖ Garrett Wesner

Most reservists, regardless of their level of adaptability amid the sea changes in their lives, talk of one or two negative changes to their personality, such as shortness of temper, a lack of patience, intolerance for "stupid" civilian behaviors, a developed prejudice against anyone who looked or sounded "Middle Eastern," or the fear of confined or crowded spaces. Others talked of binge drinking, developing a crass use of foul language, or losing religious faith. Among the more adaptive reservists of the previous chapter, these conditions, when experienced, were transient and dissipated within a couple of weeks of returning home. For the struggling soldiers, at least one of these problems lingers. In the case of young enlistee Garrett Wesner, however, a multitude of troubles punctuates his life, and throughout our ninety-minute conversation, he oscillates between the happy-go-lucky guy he wants to be and the short-tempered, crass-talking man he has trouble suppressing. As a self-described "country boy," Garrett seems like he would be comfortable driving a pickup truck to a stockcar race with Garth Brooks playing on the radio in the background. Despite his difficulties, Garrett loves being a soldier and looks fondly on his time during both deployments. Like Lionel Johnson, many of Garrett's struggles are home-grown. Throughout his deployments, his mother in particular constantly needed his emotional support. He rubs his hands through his light brown hair and explains,

> It's funny, 'cause she's a grown woman—she's forty-five years old, but at the same time she leans on me probably as much as I lean on her. She's in the middle of her second divorce that happened while I was deployed, so, I mean, emotionally, I know she's very needy of my support.

At one point her relationship with her estranged second husband had become such a crisis that the company commander flew Garrett home to be with her. His mother's marital problems clearly continue to weigh heavily on his mind, but as he talks about the situation, Garrett dances around the specifics, unable to confront the problem in its entirety.

While Garrett knows that his family life adds stress to his experiences, he also feels that the process of serving in Iraq has changed him in some fairly negative ways:

> I'm surprised that I'm this way because nothing *too* traumatic happened to us, and I'm just—and I know I'm not the same person. I just can't really point out why or how, and we've as—a small group of us have had conversations about this, I'm sure, like, and pretty much what I say, they say. I'm short with people. I have no tolerance for people, you know, like I've started drinking a lot more, which I can't believe I can do that. . . .
>
> I'm just not—I'm not happy. I used to be, live for life. I want to experience and enjoy as much of it as I can, and I could just give a shit any more. I mean, there's things that I like that I'm going to do that have always been close to me, and there's a few things that I haven't done that I want to be that I will do. But besides that, there's not much more motivation for me to make an effort for anything. I mean, I don't know how to put a word on it or explain it—just inside, I don't feel like me. And I know I've slowly been getting some of that back— I mean, my sense of humor has changed to make people laugh again for the most part, not to be mean. But every once in a while there's a

slip. But I just don't feel happy. . . . And my whole life I've been a happy person.

And then, I go overseas, I go to Iraq, I have that ripped from me. What I feel was my soul was torn out of me. . . . I don't feel like I used to . . . and it just—I hurt inside. And I don't know why 'cause I truly believed in what I was doing. I would go over [to Iraq again] in a snap of my thumb, you know, if they said, "I need people to lead soldiers. Do you want to go?" As much as my boss would hate it, my mom would hate it, even the ex, who is still a friend of mine, would hate it, I would go in a heartbeat. Just because I know my experience can help save at least one soldier. I mean, it just rips you apart and it destroys who you are.

And the only people I'm happy and comfortable around are these soldiers here. 'Cause they're the only people who really and truly understand what I went through. And I didn't go through anything, but at the same time I did—I mean, I've lost more friends being home from over there than I had when I was over there.

Our conversation with Garrett took place eight months after his return, and he was still struggling to find himself. Although Garrett believes that he is slowly getting back to being himself, it is indeed a prolonged process in the absence of clear military guidance.

Coming home, the support we get when we first get home is tremendous. It's the support that we need later that's lacking. And I truly believe that no matter who gets elected, it's going to be a long road. . . . It's not over for reservists and National Guardsmen, and they're going to need support when they're home farther down the road than three days. They're going to need three months, six months, nine months, twelve months, fifteen months. They're going to need that, and I truly believe it's up to the military to help out because not all of us have the resources to do it on our own.

Coping with Homegrown and War-Zone Struggles

When we entered the lives of the members of the 893rd six months after their homecoming, several of the reservists regarded our conversations

with them as cathartic moments. Garrett Wesner was one of several soldiers to speak specifically on this point:

> I must say, it is nice to be able to talk to you as a third person because
> it's a different perspective. Because I can talk to these guys because
> they were there and everything, and I can talk to my mom and my ex-
> girlfriend, but they were involved in it as it happened. I can talk to my
> friends, but I wrote them and told them about it while I was there. I
> can sit here and talk to you that I don't know from Adam, and I can
> vent anything I want and get it off my chest. . . . And it's nice to have
> that. And even setting up somebody like this to talk to that even with-
> out you doing your study, just having someone to sit and talk to, a
> third person that's not involved in the military, an outside person, be
> it a doctor, be it a priest, be it some student that wants to get their feet
> wet. It's nice.

Throughout our visits to the reserve center buildings that house the
893rd and several other military reserve companies, we received access
to all public spaces as well as many private spaces. Posted within the
reserve centers were a variety of official army notices regarding policies
and procedures. Posters or pamphlets reminded soldiers of issues such
as what constitutes sexual harassment, the procedures and regulations
for random drug testing, how to apply for college funding benefits,
appropriate military dress uniforms for both men and women, maps of
the army chain of command with accompanying insignias, and eight-
by-ten glossy photos of President George W. Bush and Secretary of
Defense Donald Rumsfeld. No one seemed to notice that absent from
the walls or bulletin boards were any notifications about when, where,
or how to seek help with the problems associated with either homegrown or war-zone struggles.[9]

We ended our conversational interviews by asking the reservists
what policy they would suggest the army implement in regard to
reserve service. One of the most common responses was a call for more
opportunities to meet, as Garrett suggests, with trained chaplains or
counselors to simply talk things over. The military provided debriefing
training for the reservists both at Ft. McHenry and in Kuwait prior to
the unit's return from Iraq. Still, back at their reserve centers, a sizable

group of soldiers continue to struggle to sort through their troubles while feeling as though they have few official resources available to guide them or their civilian networks through the new terrains of their lives.[10] The ability to settle firmly back onto solid civilian ground is also hampered by the uncertainty they feel in knowing, despite having served two years of deployments, they may be jerked back into the war at any moment.

six

New Conscripts of the Twenty-first-Century U.S. Army

"Obviously They Have No One Else"

I actually got to the point where I felt like the army was going to use me until I died, as in died while I was doin' my job. Because after being deployed once and being deployed again, I was like, "So, obviously they have no one else. So they're just going to continue to deploy me until I get killed in action, and then obviously I can't be deployed again because I'm dead." And I really felt that way a lot of times. I was like, "What? They'll probably deploy me a third time."

— *Enlisted Army Reservist Troy Bixler*

Troy Bixler may be prophetic in his concern that the U.S. Army is running out of troops available for deployment relief in Iraq and that he and other members of the 893rd may again be remobilized to go overseas to fight. In December 2006, the army's chief of staff, General Peter J. Schoomaker, told the Commission on the National Guard and Reserve that if current military policy was not soon altered, "we will break the active component."[1] Schoomaker, like the generals in his position since the founding of the United States, must ponder and solve the problem of how to raise an army during protracted wars when public opinion sobers. With the drafting of civilians taken off the board since the end of the Vietnam War, Schoomaker outlined three options. One is to reduce the demand on the army. However, the general is hardly sanguine about this option, given that the wars in Iraq and Afghanistan will require very robust use of ground forces well into the future.[2] The two remaining options, both endorsed by the general, are to increase substantially the size of the active-duty army, a recruiting and training process that takes years, or to mandate that units of the National Guard and Army Reserve that have already been deployed to Iraq and Afghanistan be redeployed, a political process available with the stroke of a pen.[3] Within a matter of weeks, the newly appointed secretary of defense, Robert M. Gates, took up that pen and announced changes in Pentagon policy that enable National Guard and Reserve units that have served in Iraq and Afghanistan to be recalled for another tour of duty. The rule changes are designed so that units may be recalled "without having to issue another politically delicate mobilization order."[4]

Is it reasonable to designate army reservists to fill the gap in the U.S. Army's manpower needs for a protracted land war on foreign soil that has lost favor with the civilian public? Through 2006, the members of the 893rd are among only fifty-six thousand Reserve soldiers who have served in multiple deployments since 9/11, including one full tour of duty in Iraq.[5] Moreover, they have been deployed involuntarily as a company, the preferred means of military planners, rather than as individual volunteers who move into vacant positions in already deployed units. In this context, drawing on the perspectives of the members of the 893rd, we put forward the notion that reservists are becoming the new conscripts of the twenty-first-century U.S. Army. While 9/11 propelled reservists in the 893rd to accept the call to duty, nearly all feel strongly that they have fulfilled their obligations to the country. Moreover, the great majority of the reservists distrust any promises about their future in the military. Few express a desire to go back to Iraq; in fact, one cluster of reservists would likely rebel against such an order or muster out of the military completely by whatever legitimate means possible were they to be redeployed.[6] These soldiers, whom we call resistant reservists, have characteristics that may be highly valuable to the army yet are unlikely to be available for redeployment or as a pool of new army recruits.

Resistant Reservists

While initially shocked by the shift in their military status from part-time reservists to full-time deployed soldiers, adaptive and struggling reservists alike ultimately came to embrace their new identities as soldiers. In thinking retrospectively about their pre-9/11 lives, the members of the 893rd typically identified themselves as primarily citizens who made a part-time commitment to national service. As citizen-soldiers, the emphasis of identity is placed on the civilian rather than military aspects of their lives. As events unfolded following 9/11 and these men and women were called to active duty not once but twice, they came to embrace the increased demands placed on them as soldiers and began to resonate with their soldier identity. While most of these reservists have no desire to be recalled to active duty and go back to Iraq, they would likely answer such a call for extraordinary service. But what of those reservists who spent their deployments trying desperately to hold onto their civilian identities and who had doubts about the Iraq War from the outset?

These young men—and they were all men—may have received all the love and support in the world from parents, girlfriends, fiancées, fellow students, faculty members, employers, and church members, but this support only underscored their feelings of being in the wrong place or wrong war at the wrong time. All had initially signed up for reserve duty, in part because of a sense of duty to the country. College money would help as well, but they wanted to give something back to the country as they pursued their dreams for prosperous civilian lives. As the war in Iraq has drawn on, this small group of resistant reservists wrestles with the larger implications of having served in a war waged under false pretenses.

❖ Brad Whitman

As part of the immediate post-9/11 buildup to secure military bases and
key strategic targets, junior NCO Brad Whitman was called to his first
deployment within hours of the attacks on the World Trade Center and
the Pentagon. This would be the first of three consecutive deployments
that interrupted his college studies over the next two years. Dressed in
his BDUs and with his blond hair poking out from under his beret,
Brad, at least from the exterior, looks like a natural-born soldier.
Beneath this facade, however, is a person deeply conflicted by his role in
the "global war on terror." While a patriot at heart with a deep love of
his country, Brad talks of the difficulty of being a politically liberal soldier in what he sees as the Bush administration's war:

> It was a more personal struggle for me while I was there, not for so
> many other people because most of the majority of your military per-
> sonnel are your Pat Buchanan or G. Gordon Liddy fanatics. But for
> me and a few others, it was a more personal level of you got this feel-
> ing like we're here for definitely the wrong reasons. So I think it was a
> little bit more involved for some of us than most of us.

When asked whether the war was worth his personal sacrifices, Brad's
eye twitches with stress as he exhales a long sigh and replies sadly,

> This is the fight that I bring to bed *every* night. I cannot give you a
> definite answer. One day I can say, "Yes, we made a difference. Yes, we
> were there with a purpose. Yes, we helped." But then the next day, I
> can tell you, "No, we probably pissed more off [more people] than
> what we—we probably did worse than when we"—I don't know. I
> would hate to think that I walked away with sacrificing something for
> nothing. I don't know. It's just I haven't answered that question for
> myself.

Brad's struggle to find peace within his new veteran status not only
stems from having felt like a liberal soldier fighting in an unjust war but
is compounded by the stressful circumstances of serving in a war zone.

Although he tries to be an optimistic person, his voice takes on an edge as he describes his continued struggles with the fog of war:

> The worst thing that I'm going to have to live with the rest of my life is whether or not I killed somebody. That's the bottom line. I don't know. . . . I'm not going to sit here in front of you, and I'm not going to say that everything's fine, it's great, I'm back on track . . . because I'd be lying to you. And it's not because I don't—I mean, transitioning back to civilian life—I mean, now I'm fighting my, now I'm fighting like personal views with what's going on. I'm fighting and trying to balance both, and it's hard. I know something's wrong, and I know that three or four hours of sleep a night is not [enough], but this has been going on I don't know how long. Having night sweats. I wake up and I don't remember anything, but there's gotta be something wrong. I mean I set my air-conditioning like fifty-two degrees, so there's gotta be something wrong, but I don't know, you know. It scares me, I think. I think that's the bottom line.

Other, more adaptive soldiers sometimes speak of the need for a soldier to disconnect his or her individual military job or mission from the larger picture of the geopolitical conditions that bring them to war. Such soldiers take comfort in knowing that they are doing a good job of performing the work they have been ordered to do. However, resistant soldiers could not disconnect their service to the country from the politics of the war. Their assessment of the situation includes the belief that the Iraq War increased rather than undermined the threat of international terrorism and that the war is unjust.

❖ Troy Bixler

Like Brad Whitman, enlistee Troy Bixler is a college student and patriot who grew disillusioned with the army over the course of his deployments. At first pass, Troy comes across in conversation with the air of confidence displayed by so many of the adaptive soldiers, but no matter how many times he lifts his chest forward to stress a key point or pounds his fist on the table for emphasis, lurking behind this curtain of confidence is a young man deeply troubled by the level of sacrifice he has made. Smallish in stature, he looks like he would be much more comfortable carrying a backpack to classes than an M-16 into a war zone, but as the son of a former military man, Troy eagerly anticipated military service growing up and embraced his basic training. His enthusiasm for soldiering diminished considerably as he questioned the purpose of his deployments throughout his time both at Ft. McHenry and in Iraq and struggled through to maintain his civilian identity:

> When I came out of basic, I definitely saw myself as a soldier. Oh, yeah—I was like on top of the world. I've gone through all this high-speed training. It's all hard-core. You're like a rock-hardened individual coming out of training. You're brainwashed to do whatever the army wants you to do. I don't say brainwash in a negative fashion. It is a positive thing, 'cause you need it. You need it for when you go to the real combat zones. . . .
>
> But for being on active duty for two years and seeing what active-duty life is here in the United States as well as overseas, I definitely prefer the civilian life and will stick with it. . . . I see myself more as a citizen. Even when I was on active duty, I tried to see myself as a citizen, even though sometimes it made my road more difficult because when you're [mobilized to] active duty, you have to be in active-duty mode, okay, which is you're a soldier twenty-four hours a day, seven days a week. But I would take every opportunity that I could to be a citizen even if I was overseas or whatever because the army is not a career for me. And for people who it is, that's fine. I don't mind that at all. We need people who make career soldiers, but, no, I definitely see myself more of a citizen. Even when I show up here [at drill], I'm all civilianized, and I know, like, I catch myself when it's appropriate to be a soldier. You know, I know when I should throw out the rank instead of just saying by their first name or whatever. I know when to be appropriate. It's just that I'll get away with as much civilian as I can while I'm here. So I definitely look at myself as being more of a civilian.

Troy considers himself to be a bit of a military history buff, so his expectations for the level of service typically demanded of reservists are grounded in research. By the time he returned from Ft. McHenry and restarted his college studies, Troy had completely lulled himself into believing that the army could not possibly call on his unit again after the soldiers had already sacrificed a year. This mind-set only increased his anger and disappointment when the recall came:

> It was just the fact that they were deploying me, period. That really made me upset. I didn't even think that it was possible for them to deploy me so shortly after. I was so surprised when I got the orders again, because up until this point reservists had been deployed for a maximum of nine months. It's the way it's been for the like the last fifty years, you know, and they deploy us for a year and I'm like, "Okay, no way. It can't happen again. That was a whole year, that's like longer than any reservists did in the last thirty, fifty years, you know." Then five months later—Boom, out the door again. I was like, "No way." And so a lot of it was shock, too. I couldn't believe it. I was in denial the whole time.

Troy tries to argue that the company's mission in Iraq was worth his personal sacrifices, but in doing so, he ends up making a relatively angry point that the demands placed on reservists are at odds with a domestic culture engaged in conspicuous consumption and an increasing separation from the wars in Afghanistan and Iraq:

> I'd have to say that a citizen-soldier, one word to sum it all up is *sacrifice*. . . . As a soldier, when you go overseas—or anywhere for that matter, deployed even homeland—you're not there for you. Holy smokes—I wasn't there for me. I was there for the three hundred million American citizens that are sitting in the country sucking on their chocolate milk at night and watching the *Flintstones* on their television.

Rather than strictly bracketing his deployments as a lived experience or regarding his service as making a difference in the "global war on terrorism," Troy's reflections place his soldiering in the context of what he sees as a sequence of American foreign policy blunders and squandering of power.

I view American foreign policy a little differently. I view the army in general a little differently. If you've ever read the book *Another Century of War.* . . . You have a century of war, then another century of war, and [the book] shows you how American foreign policy—it's hard for me to say, but in a lot of cases has been one blunder after another. That's just the best way to put it. America has a lot of power, so we do have a great responsibility to other nations. Because the Spiderman line is perfect—"With great power comes great responsibility." But we really botch our foreign policy. I mean, I can give you examples from Iran to Iraq to Afghanistan to even way back in the day when we were dealing with Vietnam and all the way back to World War II, though that was actually one of our better foreign policy maneuvers.

Having been called unexpectedly to engage in a war on foreign soil, resistant reservists such as Troy Bixler and Brad Whitman at least hoped to serve in a war that had positive outcomes. They ultimately remain unable to convince themselves, try as they may, that the U.S. involvement in Iraq was worth their sacrifices as citizen-soldiers. Given the failure to bring about a peaceful transition to democracy and the continued unrest in Iraq, the internal struggles of these men are wrapped around negative judgments about the policies that put them on the ground in Iraq.

These resistant reservists represent only a small group of the members of the 893rd we came to know. However, we strongly suspect that the 893rd and similar units have many more such resistant reservists. After returning from Iraq, many members of the 893rd who were eligible for discharge or retirement took advantage of that option and left the army altogether. Still other company members simply did not attend drill weekends and were essentially absent without leave.[7] Reservists present at the drill weekends often referred to their discharged or absent colleagues through stories and language suggesting that these veterans had grown weary or disgusted with the army.[8] Surprisingly, their absence is accepted more than it is resented, probably, we suspect, because they did their jobs effectively while deployed. Resistant reservists such as Troy and Brad have many attributes that are valuable to today's military. They are ambitious, analytical, more educated than many of their peers, and patriotic. In a protracted ground war that lacks substantial support in the civilian sphere, it is likely that these citizen-soldiers will muster out of the reserves by any legitimate means afforded to them formally or through more informal means enabled by their home units. Moreover, we doubt that citizens with these traits will come forward as much as they did prior to or just after 9/11 despite even greater material incentives now available to new recruits.[9]

Ironically Conscripted

Resistant reservists highlight what we see as a harsh irony of total force policy—those who volunteered as citizen-soldiers for part-time military service have become the conscripts of the wars in Iraq and Afghanistan. Their lives are no longer their own to live. Nick Trimble, an adaptive reservist who lost his self-employed civilian business through the deployments, puts this issue most succinctly when he states, "As a citizen, I try to think years ahead, but as a soldier, just day by day." The most common theme expressed by adaptive, struggling, and resistant reservists is a growing sense of frustration at living under the specter of uncertainty. Glenn Adams, the adaptive senior NCO who retired after more than twenty years of service, reveals the utter confusion about President George W. Bush's and the Pentagon's interpretation of twenty-four months of reserve service during war:[10]

> I think the biggest thing that needs to be cleared up is the whole—the true definition of our twenty-four-month [service]. Because no one can show it to even me in writing exactly what it is, and that's one of those things, different places you read it, people have interpreted it differently. But nobody's willing to do that. And, again, I don't know if it's because they are afraid they may need to bend that rule a little bit or what it is, but even the recruiters have been asking because they get asked that question all the time. And no one can give them the actual policy. I mean it's written in Title 10, but Title 10 actually does not say anything about a change in mission name. And I haven't been able to find anything, but that's what's always told to us. If they change the

mission, they can call you up for another twenty-four months, but I have not seen that in writing. No one can show it to me in writing. The only thing I see in writing is that if there was a full mobilization, they can call you back. In other words, if World War III breaks out, they can call you back. So, just things like that that even people at my level don't understand, then there's no way [lower-ranking] people can understand.

As Glenn's comments indicate, citizen-soldiers, regardless of rank or time in the army, are confused about the possibility of serving additional deployments. While they know on one level that somewhere within their military contracts they are supposed to be guaranteed no more than two years of deployment status within a five-year time frame, they have difficulty believing that a military, stretched increasingly thin, will hold up its end of the bargain. While some contemplate transferring to active-duty status, many others have grown more distrustful and distant from a military that initially seemed appealing materially and culturally. These men and women now live with a lack of certainty for the future, looking over their shoulders to see if the military might call their number one more time for involuntary deployment. In this regard, they have become the new conscripts of the twenty-first-century U.S. Army.

By early 2007, the war in Iraq hit a milestone. U.S. troops had served as long in Iraq as they had in World War II—four years.[11] If World War II comparisons are to be made, then we might also think about the level of civilian involvement in the war effort. World War II was marked by the enlistment—both voluntary and involuntary—of more than sixteen million men and women in the armed services. Civilian jobs left behind were occupied by women previously held outside of the labor market, and the popular image of Rosie the Riveter served as a civilian rallying cry for women's national service. War bonds were sold, children ran scrap metal drives, gasoline and certain foods were rationed, and families sacrificed conspicuous consumption.

In contrast, the overwhelming burdens of the wars in Iraq and Afghanistan have fallen disproportionately on our all-volunteer military force, the combination of professional soldiers, National Guards-men, and reservists numbering today approximately 2.4 million. For those keeping track of numbers, the U.S. population in 1940 was a little over 132 million; today, that number tops 300 million. At the time of World War II, a little more than 12 percent of the population served in the military, compared to less than 1 percent today. In an effort to main-tain key troop positions, as early as September 14, 2001, "the President invoked his power 'to suspend certain laws relating to promotion, involuntary retirement, and separation of commissioned officers' and delegated that power to the Secretary of Defense," thus initiating a series of "stop-loss policies" that allowed the army to "retain personnel possessing select skills 'on active duty beyond their date of retirement, separation, or release from active duty for an open-ended period.'"[12] Although no one in the 893rd was subject to the stop-loss policies, this maneuver looms large for the reservists and heightens their skepticism. Troy Bixler does little to hide his disgust with the changes in military policy and the heavy price reservists are paying:

> It makes me so angry to think that the army feels that it has the right to extend people's contracts and hold them past their original orders. Who do they think they are? And there's nothin' you can do about it, you know. And then what happens is if you talk to people higher up in the chain, you'll get this brainwash rhetoric that they just spew end-lessly, and it's almost like they try to put aside the fact that people are flesh and blood and have heart and soul, you know. "Oh, it's your duty and mine." I have already had people, you know, asking me from inside the army, you know, "Why aren't you gonna reenlist?" Oh, blah, blah, blah, you know, trying to make you feel bad. Like you haven't done enough for your country. Yet the army's only 1.2 million people. There are 300 million people in America. Look at the percent-age of people in the service right now, and yet even in the army they try to make you feel like you haven't done enough if you tell them you're not going to reenlist. I'm just, like, that's so wrong. . . . They can break their own laws, their own regs. They do it all the time. Con-tracts? They break 'em all the time. Hold people in, so. I know they can. And it is unfortunate because you have to hold up to your end of the bargain, but they don't have to hold up to theirs.

Even the well-adapted soldiers are highly anxious about returning to Iraq. Lane Wright is proud of his service and stands ready to do more soldiering—as long as it is not back in Iraq.

> Well I definitely don't want to go again. . . . I just don't like the idea of possibly having to go back, so if there was any policy I would prefer, I would like the security of knowing that I did my time in Iraq, I don't have to go back. But 'cause that's what I worry about. Heck, I don't want to go back. But that's what scares me. If I could go back and go to the same place doin' the same thing I was doin', fine because I was pretty happy doin' that. But 'cause there's stuff over there that I wouldn't want to do. Like I said, I didn't want to leave the prison camp. I didn't like to go on convoys, and I used to tell my buddy, I said, "These guys that go through the city kicking in doors and searching and patrolling, I don't want to do that." I have no desire at all, and there's obviously people that—I could even send a guy in here for you that that's what he wanted to do. He wants the action. So that's the biggest fear about going back is I don't want to. It seems like it's gotten a little worse on TV, which, like I said, I don't put too much into what I see on TV, but, yeah, I don't want to go back. That's what I want. There's been such a turnover, too. I don't want to take this group back just 'cause, one, I don't know half of them; two, the average age dipped way down now. I wouldn't mind doin' another deployment if the army needed me, but I don't want to go back to Iraq. I'd be happy to go anywhere else. Well, what I mean, I don't want to go to Afghanistan either.[13]

The Legacy of Total Force

In March 2006, a full three years after the U.S. invasion of Iraq, we talked with college juniors and seniors about our project. The spring academic semester was winding down, and graduation was less than two months away for the many seniors in the audience. We began our discussions by posing a question: "Assuming wars need to be fought— and yes, for the pacifists among us, that is a big assumption—but, assuming wars need to be fought, who should fight them?" The audience members seemed a bit taken aback by the question as they pondered the possibilities. With the exception of one young man who was already a member of the National Guard, these were students who enjoyed the benefits of being at a small, private liberal arts institution without the cost of military service, and such service was not on their radar for postgraduation career moves. After talking among themselves, the audience members came up with two main answers to our question. First, they stated what seemed like an obvious answer: the people who fight the wars should be the ones who *want* to fight in wars, those who volunteer for military service. Second, and equally telling of their general sentiment about the desirability of military service, they suggested that military service would be a good option for our nation's prisoners. After all, they reasoned, the prisoners were not serving society in any productive manner, so perhaps they could be drafted into military service.[14] As young men and women who grew up under the total force policy of the all-volunteer armed services, their projected ambivalence or distancing of themselves from the concept of national military service should not be surprising, even if their reasoning about drafting incarcerated people is very disturbing.

The question of how to raise armies is certainly not new. Temporary troops are typically raised either by obtaining volunteers through a variety of incentives or by a government-orchestrated conscription of a selective or universal service.[15] At this nation's founding, George Washington advocated that "every Citizen who enjoys the protection of a free government, owes not only a proportion of his property, but even of his personal services to the defense of it."[16] While Washington's ideal was reflected in the conceptualization of the Militia Act of 1792, which called for "universal liability for service, with few exceptions, among able-bodied white male citizens between the ages of eighteen and forty-five," never has a system of national service been created that did not provide a loophole for those with the means to opt out.[17] While the history of the U.S. military flows from the ideals of potential universal voluntary service to the practice of conscripting young men disadvantaged by economic and cultural forces into wars throughout the first three-quarters of the twentieth century, the findings of the Gates Commission effectively ended the draft in July 1973.[18] During his 1972 Senate hearings for confirmation to the position of chief of the army, General

Creighton Abrams was grilled primarily on the particulars of combat and air strike activities in Vietnam. When the conversation turned to the composition of the anticipated all-volunteer army following the impending end of the draft, the senators focused their questions on the racial makeup of the army and ways in which General Abrams might address the racial tension within the ranks. No one asked a single question about the anticipated role of the reserve component, and Abrams finally volunteered, "We have got a problem on Reserve component training." He then continued,

> The Active Army is smaller now, resulting in greater readiness demands upon reserve forces than before, thereby creating problems for the Reserve Components both in the short and the long terms. . . . In a word, the Reserve Components are suddenly being faced with greatly increased expectations following years in which national policy has relegated them to a rather passive, secondary role, while at the same time the Active Army was expanding through use of the draft.[19]

While military policymakers and analysts understood this paradigmatic shift, the same cannot be said for the public consciousness. Martin Binkin and William Kaufmann of the Brookings Institution warned in 1989, "This unprecedented dependence on the reserves has been instituted with little public fanfare or debate, yet the consequences could be dramatic and far-reaching."[20] Abrams's cautionary note about total force has, of course, become reality, and as early as September 2003, Lieutenant General James R. Helmly, chief of the Army Reserve, explained the paradigmatic shift in the use of reserve forces:

> Army Reserve soldiers have been deployed 10 times in the past 12 years for operations from Bosnia to Iraq. During the 75 years before that, the Army Reserve had been mobilized just nine times. Since December 1995, we have been in a continuous state of mobilization, with an average of nearly 9,300 soldiers mobilized each year. The years after Sept. 11 have seen more than 80,000 Army Reserve soldiers mobilized to fight the global war on terrorism. . . . In fact, the term "weekend warrior" hardly applies.[21]

While reserve call-ups were intended to help put a stop to military adventurism on the part of politicians and engage the sympathies of the broad American public, the policy seems to fall short of that goal. Many critics of the end of conscription, military sociologist Morris Janowitz among the most vocal, warn of the strong potential for a widening disconnect between the military as a social institution and the civilian sector.[22] In arguing against an all-volunteer force, Janowitz cautioned policymakers that relying on an economic model that treats military service as part of the competitive labor force only increases the army's reliance on a very narrow band of the American public. In the recent documentary film *Why We Fight,* former Pentagon analyst and whistleblower Franklin Spinney underscores the danger of dismissing the repeated price paid by mobilized reserve and active-duty soldiers because they are all volunteers:

> Right now you have more of a separation between the military and particularly the middle class and the upper middle class in this country than existed even under the draft era. If you go back to Vietnam, basically the inequity of the draft helped prolong the war. As long the poor and unrepresented were dying, people went along with it. You know we got out of Vietnam effectively when the lottery was started and middle-class kids were dying. The first thing that happened is they moved to an all-volunteer army. And that solved the inequity problem because everyone is a volunteer. . . . And that makes the military much easier to use. Because, you know, "You guys are fucking volunteers, screw you. You signed up for this." You know, the objections don't carry as much water.

As we communicated to friends and colleagues who, like ourselves, have made few if any sacrifices since 9/11 our view that citizen-soldiers are becoming the new conscripts of the twenty-first-century U.S. Army, we heard a similar refrain—these guys *volunteered* for military service, they have received the benefits, including money for college, that go with signing up, and now they should be expected to fulfill their duties. Other friends and colleagues, particularly those who have served in the military, worry that calling veteran reservists *conscripts* denigrates their patriotism and willingness to endure extreme sacrifices for the rest of us. Our designation of them as conscripts is intended to awaken the public to their sacrifices and draw the attention of decision makers to halt the abuse of reservist call-ups to sustain protracted wars that are neither just nor in the interest of the United States. We as researchers have the luxury of bringing this book project to an end point even as the wars in Iraq and Afghanistan continue. This is not the case for the reservists of the 893rd and all citizen-soldiers, whether currently demobilized at home or deployed in military theaters around the world, who must continue to live under the specter of uncertainty about when or how their extraordinary sacrifices will end.

Afterword

We present the experiences of the men and women of the 893rd in the present tense. We are keenly aware that this grammatical choice creates a false sense of time and in essence freezes the reservists in the period of our conversations with them. In reality, of course, the negotiation of military and civilian demands for these citizen-soldiers did not come neatly to some conclusion as we drew our interview process to a close. Some of the members of the 893rd volunteered for peacekeeping missions in areas such as Haiti in hopes of gaining some sense of control over their military destinies and of avoiding another possible deployment to Iraq. Other unit members continued to struggle with strained family relationships until those relationships ultimately frayed beyond repair. Others have tried to put their deployment time behind them and move forward in active pursuit of civilian goals. Still others have rejected the military's efforts at retention and have run out their military contracts, receiving honorable discharges. All should be remembered for the sacrifices they have made since 9/11, when the U.S. Army finally implemented its total force policy and embarked on what it thought would be a more effective way of raising and maintaining its ground forces in a protracted foreign war. Perhaps the greatest discontent of these men and women should rest not in that they have been called to extraordinary service but that so many of the rest of us have been allowed to avoid it.

Appendix A
Frames, Logic, and Methods of Inquiry
Giving Voice to Citizen-Soldiers

I'm not the same—well, I'm the same person that went to Iraq—I'm not the same person that was in Iraq. . . . I think, when I went to Iraq, when I first went to Iraq, I was the person I am now, always joking, laughing. When I was in Iraq, it was kinda a different place, different time. I wasn't always joking as much as I usually do and just wasn't sayin' all the stuff I would, I guess, normally say in an everyday kinda situation 'cause I guess it was more stressful. But now that I'm back, I'm back to the same old person I used to be, so, jokin' all the time and whatnot.
                                        —*Enlisted Army Reservist Vanessa Hendricks*

Vanessa Hendricks joined the 893rd just prior to the company's Iraq deployment. In addition to being a wartime reservist, she is a college student in her early twenties who loves spending time in the outdoors, traveling, playing softball, working with children, and hanging out with family members. While deployed to Iraq, she says she was a different person than she was before going and since returning. We sat down with her six months after returning from Iraq, and in a conversational interview, Vanessa ticked off her demographic identity and talked at length with us about how who she is shifts over time given the circumstances of her life. Vanessa was a soldier under stress in Iraq, but she also held onto her close family ties through telecommunication, bonded with other women in her unit, and contrasted her experiences in Iraq with her life as a young, single, female college student. Vanessa reports that she has made a smooth transition back to her civilian life and is once again a pretty happy-go-lucky college student.

Vanessa and all of the reservists we interviewed reveal unique stories about how their senses of themselves and their relational dynamics evolved before, during, and after their post-9/11 deployments. At the same time, each story adheres to the stories of other fellow reservists in the 893rd. Finding these clusters of individuals is substantially a bottom-up process of interpretation in which some reservists appear to have life stories that parallel one another yet also diverge significantly from the stories of others who served in the same company, under the same command, and doing the same military missions.

As these clusters became apparent to us over time, we named them, even as the process of naming came only after considerable dialogue between us and many readings of their life stories. Vanessa is in a cluster we call **adaptive reservists,** who adjust quickly, moving lockstep with changing institutional expectations as a result of a dynamic sense of their identity and relational networks that run deep at home and in the military. Depicted in chapter 4, these reservists cut across gender groups and include men who have experienced international deployments and all the female soldiers who were raised in military families. Another grouping, which we call **struggling reservists,** has troubles that are more homegrown than a product of their war-zone experiences and many have unreasonable expectations of those who are significant in the networks of their civilian lives. Many of these reservists, featured in chapter 5, burrow themselves in their deployments, and nearly all are males who express their views about war and relationships in masculine terms. Most occupy the lower rungs of the American workforce, and few have education beyond high school. A third cluster, **resistant reservists,** consists of those who resent the interruption of their civilian routines, who dismiss military life while they live it, and who are more likely to oppose the war even as they fight in it. Resistant reservists, whose stories are presented in chapter 6, are males with high civilian expectations and college anticipated or already a part of their lives.

Frames of Inquiry

We went into the field with certain frames of inquiry to aid our interpretation of the reservists' life stories. First, we decided to build on the popular designation of reservists as citizen-soldiers. With thousands of reservists and National Guardsmen deployed to Afghanistan and Iraq, the American mass media have run hundreds of stories using this signifier,[1] and the U.S. military is embracing it in advertising campaigns to encourage Americans to join the Reserve and National Guard post-9/11. *Citizen-soldier* has become the taken-for-granted designation, yet little effort has been made to fill in its meaning, particularly by giving voice to the reservists whose lives were supremely influenced by 9/11.[2] We decided to move beyond the trope of the citizen-soldier to understand how reservists have taken on the duality of being citizens and soldiers under post-9/11 wartime conditions, a period in which work in the civilian sphere is less secure, parenting includes stay-at-home dads and working moms, and the military recruits both men and women for nearly all of its tasks.

To get underneath the popular representation of reservists as citizen-soldiers, we came to the project with the view that social identity—that is, how we come to recognize ourselves and each other through group belonging—is a fluid process of engagement in everyday life shaped by critical events that interrupt our routines, places we move through and between, the multiple institutional spaces or subject positions we occupy, and the opportunities we possess to make ourselves who we are.[3] For a reservist, identity may play out as follows:

A twenty-two-year-old reservist distinguishes herself during a year in Iraq and earns a promotion to noncommissioned officer. She is back home, and after weekend drills, she stops at a grocery store in full uniform to buy food for her mom and younger sister, for whom she still has responsibilities. The grocery clerk tells her that he too served in

Iraq as a noncommissioned officer in the National Guard, and they exchange stories for a few minutes about their experiences. She leaves feeling a strong sense of belonging as a veteran soldier. She rushes home but experiences hostility from her mom, who was expecting lunch to be prepared by now. After making lunch and doing dishes, she puts on the uniform worn by dental assistants and arrives at her civilian job just in time to assist the dentist in preparing a crown for a patient. The dentist looks at his watch and points to it, reminding her of the importance of being on time, particularly because coworkers have already made sacrifices in their own lives to make up for her missing work during the nine months she was in Iraq. She recognizes her place in the office and tenuousness of her position in the domestic workforce as she heads home at the end of the workday to care for her ill mother and younger sister.

We were unable to follow the reservists through their everyday experiences before, during, and after their deployments. To arrive at the clusters of reservists identified in this volume, we initially sifted through each reservist's stories for textual clues about his or her identification with citizen life as distinct from life as a soldier. Specifically, we took as a starting point the distinction between *citizen*-soldier and citizen-*soldier,* the difference between reservists who, in their descriptions of their experiences and activities, stress the adjective rather than the noun to interpret the ways that they handle the seismic changes in their lives over time. As *citizen*-soldiers, identity is primarily anchored in the relationships and structures within civilian life, including but not limited to family, community, civilian work worlds, and education.[4] As citizen-*soldiers,* the primary identity shifts to the relationships and structures indicative of military, with its heavy demands on reservists' time, energy, activities, and emotions. Civilian relationships, jobs, and goals are placed on the back burner, and traditional conceptualizations of civilian relationships are encroached on as expressions about family are bifurcated into categories of "blood family" (traditional family members left behind) and the newly developed "army-green family" (brothers and sisters in arms).

In the literature on professional soldiers, military sociologists have written about the competing demands of what they call the "greedy institutions" of military and family.[5] As greedy institutions, both the military and family place demands on individuals not only in terms of time but also in terms of financial expectations, specific duties, values, allegiances, and emotional commitment, to name but a few.[6] Social scientists have studied the ways in which professional, full-time soldiers negotiate their identity within the competing demands of these two greedy institutions.[7] Citizen-soldiers' part-time commitment to the military—whether as direct enlistees into the reserve system or transfers from the professional side—limits the all-encompassing grip of the military to only one weekend per month and two weeks per year when there are no national emergencies. Citizen-soldiers living pre-9/11 lives were more heavily invested in family and the civilian work sector, including the importance of higher education to good jobs. However, little is known of the ways in which citizen-soldiers negotiate the competing demands of three greedy institutions as wartime military responsibilities encroach on civilian work and family life.[8]

For the members of the 893rd, most of whom were already experiencing the competing demands of a variety of family responsibilities and civilian careers, including the pursuit of full-time education, the call to active duty by the military in the face of a national crisis, with few exceptions, trumped all other institutional and personal demands. Once called to involuntary deployment under wartime conditions, many of the reservists, including those with previous active-duty experience, were surprised by the military's grip. This was particularly the case when the reservists were deployed overseas for nearly a year, living with each other in makeshift barracks. Thus, we paid particular attention to the company of soldiers living together in this place, the focus of chapter 2.[9]

We took notions of social identity and greedy institutions into the field with us to aid our interpretative capacities in interviewing, transcribing, and thinking about our conversations with the members of the 893rd. At the same time, we came to other frames of reference inductively, just as we did the groupings of soldiers as adaptive, struggling, and resistant. This was particularly the case when we focused on who among the many millions of adult American civilians become reservists and why, the subject of chapter 3. Specifically, we came to see a distinction between instrumental orientations (the importance of joining and sustaining reservist status to cope with material needs and relative disadvantage in the domestic economy) and cultural orientations (the force of military affiliation to enhance how individuals imagine and value themselves and are imagined by others). Keeping in mind the changing circumstances of people's lives, we came to recognize that the salience of these orientations often shifts over time. For, example, an individual who, while approaching the end of high school, joins to fulfill an adolescent dream to become a soldier may come to distance himself from this strong cultural orientation after having experienced multiple deployments in the face of a much more complex home life that includes being married, having stepchildren, and being a rookie correctional officer. Therefore, we trace the members of the 893rd from the point of their recollections about joining the Reserve to their accounts of becoming part of a mobilized military company that within a two-year period was deployed to a stateside post, demobilized, and sent back home within the backdrop of escalating tension between the United States and Iraq before being remobilized, deployed to Iraq, demobilized, and sent back home again. To tell this temporal story, we use the anchors of citizen and soldier identities while exploring the nuances of the way distinctive clusters of soldiers confront the expectations of competing greedy institutions and adapt to them materially and culturally.

Logic and Methods of Inquiry

I had a good sergeant, a buck sergeant in his early twenties, three stripes on his sleeves. His name was Stoney Spikes, and he came from Alabama. He had a strong face, with a big square chin, and the other men obeyed him. He kept one of his two pairs of jungle boots polished, more or less, for the inspections we occasionally endured, which were for me almost a form of combat. The other pair he left unshined, at first perhaps because he saw no sense in shining them and later on, I think, because they made him feel more like the soldier he wished he was—because a real soldier, an infantryman, a grunt, would never wear shiny boots in the bush. Spikes had gone away on leave and had run into some buck sergeants his age who had combat infantryman's badges. "They got a name for people like us, Lieutenant," he told me when he came back. His jaw hardened. The term is REMF. It stood for "Rear Echelon Mother Fucker." Spikes never seemed quite the same after he found out what real soldiers thought of soldiers like us.[10]

Tracy Kidder, a Pulitzer Prize–winning author and Vietnam veteran, tells the story about Spikes in his memoir, *My Detachment.* Kidder was a lieutenant in charge of a detachment of eight enlisted men who gathered electronic intelligence on Vietcong and North Vietnamese troops while situated inside an army brigade's fortified base camp on the edge of the coastal plain of what in 1968 was a part of South Vietnam. Kidder tells this and other stories to reveal combat infantry units' low opinion of support units and how this status infects soldiers in support units both while deployed and after they return home. Kidder says that he and other Vietnam veterans who served in support units feel a need to embellish their stories of deployment to war zones, particularly in the presence of other veterans.[11] Kidder draws meaning about soldiering and its afterlife from Spikes and other storytellers rather than analyzing their narratives as factual accounts of what happened on the ground. Our project is like Kidder's in that we focus on the sense that soldiers make of their experiences during and after war—particularly what it means to be reservists in the early twenty-first century called on to make abrupt changes in their lives, putting themselves at risk both overseas and at home. Both Kidder's memoir and our book are interpretive projects, yet ours departs from Kidder's in that it is also an empirical research project. What do we see as the defining characteristics of an interpretive research project, and how did we put our project into play through methods of inquiry?

We regard meaning making as a highly contextualized, individualistic process; therefore, we take seriously each soldier's account of becoming a reservist, being deployed, and coming home. At the same time, we expect meaning making to be loosely coupled—that is, some soldiers have similar beliefs about relationships within the company and within their civilian networks. Sometimes, we are aided in finding these clusters of soldiers by the frames of inquiry we took into the field; at other times, reservists' own concepts override ours. We seek their meanings of being reservists in a post-9/11 environment rather than trying to prove or disprove our anticipated understandings based on the frames of reference we took into the field. In short, fieldwork trumps framework, and the voices of the reservists, in the form of rich, extended narratives, take center stage as key elements of our brand of interpretative inquiry.[12]

To uncover twenty-first-century reservists' understandings of living at the cusp of military, civilian workforce, and family life in America, we employ a conversational interviewing approach along with the collection of stories. Our protocol for conversational interviewing uses a series of open-ended questions derived from the combination of our conceptual frames, the lines of inquiry each of us has long pursued, extensive reading specific to soldiering, and the ideas of a couple of insiders, former students, and friends who have served as reservists. As we anticipated, the protocol gave us opportunities to fashion a line of questioning on the fly, particular to an individual reservist, and to explore issues that are emotional. Like Joe Soss[13] and John Gilliom,[14] who study what it means to be welfare recipients in contemporary American society, we knew that our conversations would be a forum for reservists to unload in part because we "provide individuals with an audience they may rarely encounter in everyday life: attentive, encouraging, patient, willing to press on vague answers, and eager to clear up confusions."[15]

At the end of the chapter 5, on struggling soldiers, we recount a particularly emotional conversation with a reservist who seems stressed out. These experiences, while not ordinary, are part of what occurs when engaging in conversations that have emotional content and that probe people to offer fully their understandings of what they have endured. From the get-go, we decided to ask no questions that would in any way be construed as soliciting war stories, but reservists who wanted to tell tales of war did so, even as many soldiers do not want close friends and family members to ask such questions.

While we were uninviting of war stories, we used a two-stage process to elicit the reservists' stories. Since one of us, Michael, had employed storytelling to uncover the underlying normative logic of street-level decision making of state actors, we felt this logic could be built into our conversations with the reservists to get at the ways they report handling relations among themselves and those in their social networks.[16] As in that project, here we use stories to focus on how reservists process the meaning of their deployments, how they imagine themselves and their relationships in accounting for the dramatic shifts in their everyday lives. Specifically, we gave them key lines from two contrasting stories we took from the literature on soldiering and asked them to respond. Also, we simply asked them to tell us a story about their being reservists that they found particularly compelling, usually saving this request for the end of our conversations.

We conducted interviews between May 1 and September 15, 2004, approximately five to nine months following the 893rd's return from Iraq. As a result of retirements, discharges, and transfers, it is difficult to assess the actual company membership over that five-month period; however, just under half the soldiers who had served in Iraq and were still attending drill weekends agreed to work with us. (See appendix B for reservists' demographics.) Many of the reservists were quite eager to have someone show an active interest in their lives as citizens and soldiers, while others popped in for an interview as a way to kill time in the otherwise "hurry up and wait" atmosphere that seemed to punctuate their drill life. The conclusion of one interview often found three or four more soldiers sitting around outside of the conference room waiting for their turn to tell their stories.

We typically conducted the interviews in either a vacant conference room or an unoccupied office; however, during a particularly busy weekend that involved another reserve company readying for deployment, we found a private exterior alcove that was interrupted only by the periodical passing of Humvees and equipment trucks—distracting from an interviewer's perspective but seeming to have no effect on the reservists, who had grown so accustomed to the sounds of military preparations. Our interviews lasted typically between forty-five minutes and two hours and were completely voluntary on the part of the reservists. Each interview was tape-recorded, and reservists were shown how to work the recorder prior to receiving control of the device. While most reservists spoke freely in our conversations, a few stopped the tape recorder to speak off the record or took a moment to erase a comment that in hindsight they felt was better left unsaid.

We took pains to ensure that this "special population" participated voluntarily in this project. Included among special populations are those for whom some governing body may exert subtle queues of participation expectation. Teachers hold grades over students, parents hold authority over children, prison guards hold power over prisoners, and military officers command lower-ranking soldiers. As an added precaution in working with military personnel, following a standard informed-consent process, we reminded the soldiers that the military had not contracted us to conduct this research and that they were under no obligation to participate in the project. Should they feel that somehow they had been "ordered" to participate, we could simply sit with them for a period of time and give the appearance that an interview had taken place without actually engaging in the interview process. No one took us up on this offer, and we are comfortable that those who came to us did so of their own accord with the hopes that in relaying their stories as citizen-soldiers, they might help others facing similar circumstances as well as possibly have their voices heard by current and future policymakers. As noted in the preface, pseudonyms are used throughout for all soldiers as well as the company's name and service locations.

With the conversational interviews and storytelling completed, the process of transcription marks the first step of many in the course of discovery after coming out of the field. Transcription was the beginning of our conversations of discovery, and during this process we decided that the transcripts, many of which were more than twenty single-spaced pages long, should be consolidated into what we call "life stories," or thick, chronological narratives by the reservists with only minimal transitions written by us. The life stories serve as our major tool for the later steps of interpretation and are the documents on which we draw to provide the reader with the extended narratives of the reservists that appear throughout the substantive chapters of the book. Decisions needed to be made in terms of whose voices and how many voices should be included to illustrate a point or represent an entire grouping of soldiers. For any statement made throughout the book that draws specifically on a soldier's voice, other voices could have illustrated the same point. In selecting which stories or statements to utilize, we typically worked with those that most dramatically drove the point home. We also strove to ensure that no particular soldiers became dominant within the text and that the book reads as a full chorus of voices rather than a series of a few select solos. And when we reached this point in the interpretive process and put it to word, as we did in the body of the book, we are telling our story about their stories of being reservists.[17]

Soldier Characteristics of the 893rd MP Company

TABLE B1.   Demographic Comparison between the Forty-six Participants in the 893rd Military Police Company and the Army Reserve, Fiscal Year 2004

	893rd MP Company Participants	Army Reserve 2004 Demographics[a]
Gender		
Male	89.9%	76.3%
Female	10.9	23.7
Race		
White	71.7	59.2
African American	21.7	23.8
Hispanic	4.3	10.9
Other	2.2	6.1
Rank		
Commissioned Officer	8.7	17.6
Warrant Officer	0.0	1.2
Enlisted	91.3	81.2
Marital Status		
Married	30.4	47.1
Single	56.5	n/a
Engaged	6.5	n/a
Separated	4.3	n/a
Divorced	2.2	n/a
Parental Status		
No Children	63.0	60.0
Children	37.0	40.0

[a]Total number of Army Reserve soldiers in 2004 was 204,131 (Office of Army Demographics, www.armyg1.army.mil/demographics).

TABLE B2. Additional Demographics of the Participants in the 893rd Military Police Company

Education Level		Civilian Occupation	
High School or GED	21.7%	Law Enforcement/	
Some College	56.3	Corrections/Security	34.8%
Associate Degree	6.5	College Student	17.4
Bachelor's Degree	13.0	Construction/Labor	
Graduate Degree	2.2	Technician	13.0
		White-Collar Profession	10.9
Prior Active Component		Retail	10.9
Military Service		Active Guard Reserve	4.3
Yes	28.3	Other	6.5
No	71.7	Unemployed	2.2
Pre-9/11 International			
Deployment Experience			
Yes	23.9		
No	76.1		

Note: Comparison Army Reserve data unreported

Appendix C
Glossary of Military Terminology

Abu Ghraib—Under the direction of the 800th Military Police Brigade, this prison, which was previously infamous for the inhumane treatment and torture of Iraqi citizens by Saddam Hussein, became known worldwide in April 2004 for the prisoner abuses and torture scandal at the hands of a small group of U.S. soldiers.

Army Rank Structure—The army is built on three general classifications of ranks: enlisted soldiers, warrant officers, and commissioned officers. The lowest ranks of the enlisted soldiers include privates and specialists. Noncommissioned officers are the higher-ranking enlisted soldiers who have a higher degree of responsibility: the ranks of sergeant, staff sergeant, master sergeant, and first sergeant, among others. Warrant officers hold the rank between noncommissioned officers and commissioned officers. The highest ranks of the army are commissioned officers, ranging from second lieutenants to generals.

Army Reserve and National Guard Components—The U.S. Army is divided into the active component and the reserve component. The active component comprises the soldiers employed full-time by the army. The reserve component is made up of the part-time soldiers who typically train one weekend per month and two weeks per year unless mobilized for full-time national service. The National Guard emphasizes combat training, and the Reserve units are designated primarily for combat support, ranging from running enemy prisoner of war camps to providing medical services.

Battle Dress Uniforms (BDUs)—Standard army-issued uniforms used in training exercises and combat situations alike, typically camouflaged in drab olive green for wooded environments or light tan for desert environments. BDUs differ from the formal dress uniforms used for special occasions such as parades.

Company Structure—Any military company is made up of subunits but is also a subunit of the larger military structure. Generally, about four to six companies make up a battalion. Each company typically includes about three to five platoons, each of which is under the command of a commissioned officer such as a lieutenant. In many Reserve companies, some platoons are "detached," which means that they are geographically distant from their company headquarters. Platoons are broken into squads of about ten soldiers, and the squads are broken into teams of about five soldiers.

Enemy Prisoner of War Camp (EPW)—Facilities used to detain prisoners who have surrendered to or are taken by an enemy force. Working "inside the wire" involves the actual guarding of prisoners within the prison camp facility, while working "outside the wire" involves securing the facility's perimeter and watchtowers.

Improvised Explosive Device (IED)—Also known as a roadside bomb, an IED is a generic name for a variety of explosive devices. They were among the first types of weapons used by Iraqi insurgents to disrupt coalition operations, particularly convoys.

Operation Enduring Freedom—The name of the military operation launched in response to the September 11, 2001, attacks. Commenced on October 7, 2001, with the invasion of Afghanistan in efforts to capture al-Qaeda terrorist leaders and close the country's Taliban-sanctioned terrorist training camps and infrastructure.

Operation Iraqi Freedom—Also known as the second Gulf War, Operation Iraqi Freedom is the military operation that began on March 19, 2003, to disarm Iraq of suspected, though never found, weapons of mass destruction and to remove the Iraqi regime and its dictator, Saddam Hussein, from power under the justification that Hussein was supporting al-Qaeda operations.

Operation Noble Eagle—The military operation designed for homeland security that began on September 15, 2001, with the partial mobilization of reserve troops for increased security at military installations, potential terrorist targets, and airports.

Title 10 of the U.S. Code—This is the legal authority to gain access to the reserves. There are five mobilization levels, ranging from selective mobilization to total mobilization. Congress or the president can call selective mobilization of specific reserve units and/or individuals to meet the demands of a domestic threat of safety—either a human-created or natural disaster. At the next level, the presidential selected reserve call-up, the president may call up to two hundred thousand reserve personnel for up to 270 days of service. Congress or the president may declare a national emergency and issue a partial mobilization that augments the active component with up to one million reserve soldiers for twenty-four months of service. The partial mobilization has enabled reservists to fight in the wars in Afghanistan and Iraq, and the Pentagon is currently debating what twenty-four months of service actually means. Full mobilization requires congressional action declaring a war or a national emergency and enables not only the mobilization of all reserve units but also the authorization for national conscription. Total mobilization also requires a congressional declaration of war or national emergency that devotes all national resources to sustaining or expanding the armed forces.

Notes

Introduction

1. U.S. White House, "President Holds Prime Time News Conference," October 11, 2001, http://www.whitehouse.gov/news/releases/2001/10/20011011 -7.html (accessed March 13, 2006).

2. Commission on the National Guard and Reserves, *Hearing on Proposed Changes to National Guard*, panel 2, December 14, 2006, http://www.cngr .gov/hearing121314/1214cngr-panel2.pdf (accessed April 2, 2007), 8. According to a Congressional Research Service report prepared by Lawrence Kapp for Congress on February 16, 2005, the total number of deployed citizen soldiers, including National Guardsmen, is not known since total mobilization figures count reservists more than once if they have been mobilized multiple times. See Lawrence Kapp, *Operations Noble Eagle, Enduring Freedom, and Iraqi Freedom: Questions and Answers about U.S. Military Personnel, Compensation, and Force Structure*, Congressional Research Service Report for Congress, February 16, 2005, http://fas.org/sgp/crs/natsec/RL31334.pdf (accessed April 29, 2007). Kapp estimates that "between September 11, 2001, and February 16, 2005, a total of 477,709 citizen soldiers (which includes the National Guard) were involuntarily called to active duty under *federal* orders" for Operation Noble Eagle, Operation Enduring Freedom, and Operation Iraqi Freedom (2). Again, the 477,709 includes individual soldiers who have been counted twice or more under separate deployments.

3. According to the Office of Army Demographics, for fiscal year 2004, the army consisted of 1,041,340 active duty personnel, 342,918 National Guardsmen, and 204,131 reservists. See Betty D. Maxfield, *Army Profile, FY04* (Washington,

DC: Office of Army Demographics, 2004), http://www.army91.army.mil/hr/demographics/FY04%20Army%20Profile.pdf (accessed April 10, 2007).

4. Approximately 347 soldiers of all military branches were killed in Iraq while the 893rd served its tour of duty. Of those 347 soldiers, 8 percent (28 individuals) were reservists. See Lizette Alvarez and Andrew Lehren, "Another Grim Milestone for U.S.," *New York Times,* January 1, 2007, A1, A9.

5. The gaps between these clusters of reservists are webbed with connections. All of the reservists have shared their life stories with one another in close quarters six thousand miles away from home, and as a result, they carry as part of their own stories pieces of the stories of nearly all of the rest. As academics, we are aided by concepts that we took into the field to parcel the individual stories, and as interpretive field researchers, we discovered concepts along the way that brought a loose order to the reservists' accounts. Appendix A details these concepts, or frames of inquiry, and the particulars of our method of inquiry.

6. For more information on children of military families, see Morten G. Ender, ed., *Military Brats and Other Global Nomads: Growing Up in Organization Families* (Westport, CT: Praeger: 2002).

7. Richard H. Taylor, *Homeward Bound: American Veterans Return from War* (Westport, CT: Praeger, 2007); and Richard Severo and Lewis Milford, *The Wages of War: When American Soldiers Came Home from Valley Forge to Vietnam* (New York: Simon and Schuster, 1989).

8. For discussions of the politics of posttraumatic stress disorder in relation to Vietnam veterans, see Wilbur J. Scott, *The Politics of Readjustment: Vietnam Veterans since the War* (New York: Aldine de Gruyter, 1993); Paul Starr, *The Discarded Army: Veterans after Vietnam* (New York: Charter House, 1973); Jerry Lembcke, *The Spitting Image: Myth, Memory, and the Legacy of Vietnam* (New York: New York University Press, 1998), 101–26.

9. A fuller discussion of the mixture of homegrown and war-grown struggles appears in chapter 5.

10. See CNN, "More National Guard Units May Get Second Tours in Iraq," November 11, 2006, http://www.cnn.com/2006/US/11/11/iraq.national.guard.ap/index.html (accessed November 11, 2006). See also Kapp, *Operations Noble Eagle, Enduring Freedom, and Iraqi Freedom,* 3.

Chapter One

1. Commission on the National Guard and Reserves, *Hearing on Proposed Changes to National Guard,* panel 2, December 14, 2006, http://www.cngr.gov/hearing121314/1214cngr-panel2.pdf (accessed April 2, 2007), 8. Between Operation Noble Eagle, Operation Enduring Freedom, and Operation Iraqi Freedom, the United States reached a peak of nearly 220,000 deployed Reserve and National Guard troops, constituting approximately 35 percent of all troops in Iraq. See Eric Schmitt and David S. Cloud, "The Reach of War; Troop Deployment; Part-Time Forces on Active Duty Decline Steeply," *New York Times,* July 11, 2005, A1.

2. Quoted in Larry Berman, *Planning a Tragedy: The Americanization of the War in Vietnam* (New York: Norton, 1982), 127.

3. Robert S. McNamara and Brian VanDeMark, *In Retrospect: The Tragedy and Lessons of Vietnam* (New York: Times Books, 1995), 166.

4. Reserve forces include the U.S. Army, Navy, and Air Force Reserve and the National Guard. The initial calculation was that an initial expansion of combat forces to 175,000 would require calling up 235,000 reserve forces. In this chapter, we use *Reserve* to signify American military reserve forces.

5. Quoted in Berman, *Planning a Tragedy*, 122.

6. McNamara and VanDeMark, *In Retrospect*, 201.

7. Berman, *Planning a Tragedy*, 124; see also David Halberstam, *The Best and the Brightest* (New York: Random House, 1972), 56.

8. John A. Wickham, interview by Michael Musheno and Susan Ross, May 5, 2006.

9. Berman, *Planning a Tragedy*, 127.

10. Lyndon Baines Johnson, *Vantage Point: Perspectives of the Presidency, 1963–1969* (New York: Holt, Rinehart, and Winston, 1971), 49.

11. Lawrence M. Baskir and William A. Strauss, *Chance and Circumstance: The Draft, the War, and the Vietnam Generation* (New York: Knopf, 1978), 50.

12. See Martin Binkin and William W. Kaufmann, *U.S. Army Guard and Reserve: Rhetoric, Realities, Risks* (Washington, DC: Brookings Institution, 1989), 52.

13. Wickham, interview.

14. Lewis Sorley, "Creighton Abrams and Active-Reserve Integration in Wartime," *Parameters* 21 (1991): 38. For a pre-Vietnam history of the Reserve, including deployments in World War I, World War II, the Korean War, and the Berlin Crisis, see Binkin and Kaufmann, *U.S. Army Guard and Reserve*; Richard B. Crossland and James T. Currie, *Twice the Citizen: A History of the United States Army Reserve, 1908–1983* (Washington, DC: Office of the Chief, Army Reserve, 1984).

15. Lewis Sorley, *Thunderbolt: General Creighton Abrams and the Army of His Times* (New York: Brassey's, 1998), 68–81.

16. Quoted in Sorley, "Creighton Abrams," 40.

17. Abrams's remarks, U.S. Army Judge Advocate General's School, Charlottesville, Virginia, October 1973, quoted in Sorley, "Creighton Abrams," 42.

18. Ibid., 41.

19. John R. Groves, *Crossroads in the U.S. Military Capability: The 21st Century U.S. Army and the Abrams Doctrine*, Land Warfare Papers 37 (Arlington, VA: Institute of Land Warfare, 2001), 2.

20. See Andrew Bacevich, *The New American Militarism: How Americans are Seduced by War* (New York: Oxford University Press, 2005). Bacevich argues, "Creighton Abrams's chief contribution to post-Vietnam military reforms was to begin the process of making it more difficult for civilian authorities to opt for war. That is, as Army chief of staff he took it upon himself to circumscribe the freedom of action permitted to his political masters . . . by making the active army operationally dependent on the reserves . . . no president could opt for war on any significant scale without first taking the politically sensitive and economically costly step of calling up America's "weekend warriors'" (39). Alternatively, one researcher claims that Abrams's decisions were driven solely by economic factors. See James Jay Carafano, "The Army Reserves and the Abrams Doctrine: Unfulfilled Promise, Uncertain Future," Heritage Foundation Lecture 869, paper

presented at the Foreign Policy Research Institute conference on the future of the reserves and National Guard, Philadelphia, April 18, 2005, http://www .heritage.org/Research/National Security/hl869.cfm (accessed July 27, 2007).

21. John Vessey, interview by Lewis Sorley, quoted in Sorley, "Creighton Abrams," 46.

22. Ibid.

23. Quoted in Sorley, *Thunderbolt*, 363.

24. Martin Binkin, *Who Will Fight the Next War? The Changing Face of the American Military* (Washington, DC: Brookings Institution, 1993), 111.

25. Michael Getler, "Make-Believe Mobilization Showed Major Flaws," *Washington Post*, July 14, 1980, A6.

26. Binkin, *Who Will Fight the Next War?* 103, 112.

27. Ibid., 114.

28. For an explanation of the five current mobilization levels that can be utilized to gain access to reserve forces, see U.S. Government Printing Office, "Title 10—Armed Forces," January 8, 2004, http://www.access.gpo.gov/uscode/title10/ title10.html (accessed January 15, 2006). See also Appendix C.

29. This represented 20 percent of the Army Reserve at that time. See James Griffith and Shelley Perry, "Wanting to Soldier: Enlistment Motivations of Army Reserve Recruits before and after Operation Desert Storm," *Military Psychology* 5 (1993): 127–39.

30. Lewis Sorley, "National Guard and Reserve Forces," in *American Defense Annual, 1991–1992*, edited by Joseph Kruzel (New York: Lexington, 1992), 191.

31. Quoted in ibid., 192.

32. Ibid., 193.

33. On February 25, 2001, an Iraqi scud missile hit the barracks of the 14th Quartermaster Detachment, an Army Reserve unit based in al-Khobar, a suburb of Dhahran, Saudi Arabia. The twenty-eight fatalities constituted the largest number of casualties sustained from a single attack during the first Gulf War. See Stephen M. Duncan, *Citizen Warriors: America's National Guard and Reserve Forces and the Politics of National Security* (Novato, CA: Presidio, 1996), 108.

Chapter Two

1. Among the most popular of this genre of research is Stephen E. Ambrose's *Band of Brothers: E Company, 506th Regiment, 101st Airborne from Normandy to Hitler's Eagle's Nest* (New York: Simon and Schuster, 2001), the inspiration for the popular HBO miniseries recounting of Easy Company. For books chronicling the experiences of soldiers in the current Iraq and Afghanistan Wars, see Colby Buzzell, *My War: Killing Time in Iraq* (New York: Putnam Adult, 2005); John Crawford, *The Last True Story I'll Ever Tell: An Accidental Soldier's Account of the War in Iraq* (New York: Riverhead, 2005); Nate Hardcastle and Clint Willis, eds., *American Soldier: Stories of Special Forces from Iraq to Afghanistan* (New York: Thunder's Mouth, 2002); Karl Zinsmeister, *Boots on the Ground: A Month with the 82nd Airborne in the Battle for Iraq* (New York: Truman Talley, 2003).

2. Current literature focuses on "task cohesion" (the extent to which soldiers share goals) and "social cohesion" (the extent to which soldiers like each other), both how distinguishable one is from the other and which contributes to wartime performance. See Robert MacCoun, Elizabeth Kier, and Aaron Belkin, "Does Social Cohesion Determine Motivation in Combat? An Old Question with an Old Answer," *Armed Forces and Society* 32 (2005): 1–9; Leonard Wong, Thomas A. Kolditz, Raymond A. Millen, and Terrence M. Potter, *Why They Fight: Combat Motivation in the Iraq War* (Carlisle Barracks, PA: U.S. Army War College, 2003). While we see evidence of task coherence, we are interested in relational dynamics among members of the 893rd upon deployment, or how they bond with one another and with the active-duty professional soldiers with whom they share tasks. We focus on how their bonds change over time rather than addressing the relationship between types and degrees of cohesion and performance, the focus of debate in military sociology. For a history of the development of theories of soldier group cohesion, including the classic work of Edward Shils and Morris Janowitz, see Marina Nuciari, "Models and Explanations for Military Organization: An Updated Reconsideration," in *Handbook of Sociology of the Military*, edited by Giuseppe Caforio (New York: Kluwer Academic/Plenum, 2003), 61–85.

3. Lewis Sorley, "National Guard and Reserve Forces," in *American Defense Annual, 1991–1992*, edited by Joseph Kruzel (New York: Lexington, 1992), 183–201.

4. James F. Gebhardt, "The Road to Abu Ghraib: U.S. Army Detainee Doctrine and Experience," *Military Review* 85 (2005): 47–48.

5. Ibid., 48. For complete details of the EPW operations in Operation Desert Storm, see John R. Brinkerhoff, Ted Silva, and John Seitz, *United States Army Reserve in Operation Desert Storm, Enemy Prisoner of War Operations: The 800th Military Police Brigade* (Washington, DC: Chief, U.S. Army Reserve, 1992).

6. The experiences of the 893rd are consistent with Little's work on a U.S. Army infantry unit in Korea; see Roger W. Little, "Buddy Relations and Combat Soldier Performance," in *The New Military*, edited by Morris Janowitz (New York: Sage, 1964), 195–224.

7. For discussion of issues specific to female soldiers serving in Iraq, see Sara Corbett, "The Women's War," *New York Times Magazine*, March 18, 2007, 42.

Chapter Three

1. Quoted from U.S. Army, http://www.goarmy.com/reserve/nps/index.jsp (accessed May 18, 2006).

2. Reserve recruiting campaigns also came under media attack during Operation Desert Storm. For a discussion of this issue as well as an examination of the extent to which Operation Desert Storm affected Army Reserve recruiting efforts, see James Griffith and Shelley Perry, "Wanting to Soldier: Enlistment Motivations of Army Reserve Recruits before and after Operation Desert Storm," *Military Psychology* 5 (1993): 127–39. See also Sheila Nataraj Kirby, "The Impact of Deployment on the Retention of Military Reservists," *Armed Forces and Society* 26 (2000): 259–84.

3. Quoted in David E. Rosenbaum, "Kennedy and Hatfield Disagree at Hearing on Volunteer Army," *New York Times*, February 5, 1971, 12.

4. Jeremy Arkes and M. Rebecca Kilburn, *Modeling Reserve Recruiting: Estimates of Enlistments* (Santa Monica, CA: RAND, 2005).

5. We employ here the term *cultural orientation*, which is somewhat closely aligned with Louis A. Zurcher Jr.'s conceptualization of military reserve service as occupying what he terms an ephemeral role, "a temporary or ancillary position-related behavior pattern chosen by the enactor to satisfy individual needs incompletely satisfied by more dominant or lasting roles he or she must regularly enact in everyday life positions" ("The Naval Reservist: An Empirical Assessment of Ephemeral Role Enactment," *Social Forces* 53 [1977]: 753–54).

6. Charles Moskos and Frank Wood explain the institutional/occupational (I/O) thesis, which hypothesizes that the American military historically developed as a separate institution with recruitment of membership achieved through identification with the unique mission of the military and its call to national service. More recently, and accelerated through the all-volunteer force, the military is becoming less of a distinct social institution and more characteristic of any other occupation that must compete in the regular labor market to recruit and retain membership. See Charles C. Moskos and Frank R. Wood, eds., *The Military: More Than Just a Job?* (Washington, DC: Pergamon-Brassey's International Defense Publishers, 1988); David R. Segal, "Measuring the Institutional/Occupational Change Thesis," *Armed Forces and Society* 12 (1986): 351–76. The diversity of pathways of entry to reserve service is another piece of evidence in support of the growing view of the military as an occupational choice rooted substantially in economic calculations.

7. For a discussion of the tension, for example, of deploying so many reservists from within the civilian police force, see Matthew J. Hickman, "Impact of the Military Reserve Activation on Police Staffing," *Police Chief* 73 (2006), http://policechiefmagazine.org/magazine/index.cfm?fuseaction=display_arch&article_id=1021&i ssue_id=102006 (accessed May 2, 2007).

8. Eliot A. Cohen, "Twilight of the Citizen-Soldier," *Parameters: U.S. Army War College Quarterly* 31 (2001): 23–28.

9. The metaphorical weaving of work and family is drawn from Anita Ilta Garey, *Weaving Work and Motherhood* (Philadelphia: Temple University Press, 1999).

Chapter Four

1. Often buried in research reports of soldier psychological distress and negative family functioning are less examined findings pertaining to soldier and family resilience. For example, the principal findings of Julian D. Ford, David Shaw, Shirley Sennhauser, David Greaves, Barbara Thacker, Patricia Chandler, Lawrence Schwartz, and Valerie McClain in "Psychosocial Debriefing after Operation Desert Storm: Marital and Family Assessment and Intervention," *Journal of Social Issues* 49 (1993) are "(1) the trauma and strain of war-zone military service, family separation, and subsequent family and community readjustment take a

toll on a significant minority of [Operation Desert Storm] veterans and their families that is directly related to the stress symptomatology experienced by the veteran; and (2) with timely psychosocial intervention—based on life-span developmental and self-psychology, family systems theory, and a communitarian social integration model—veterans and families in distress are able to subsequently resolve symptoms of psychosocial malfunctioning and even begin to accrue personal and systemic benefits from their ODS stressor experiences" (73). Lost in the analysis is the fact that through extensive measurement scales, the researchers identify 24 percent of the families as "high-functioning" and 50 percent as "midrange" in family functioning. Soldier and family resilience are often left unexamined; however, a recent study by James Hosek, Jennifer Kavanagh, and Laura Miller, *How Deployments Affect Service Members* (Santa Monica, CA: RAND, 2006), has acknowledged the resiliency soldiers and their families have shown through multiple deployments. This resiliency rarely appears in the popular press, as the dominant discourse focuses on veteran readjustment difficulties, whether from psychological or physical injuries. Examples abound from the *New York Times Magazine* (e.g., Scott Anderson's May 28, 2006, article, "Bringing It All Back Home") to Tom Brokaw's special report, "To War and Back" aired on NBC on December 18, 2005, in which he followed seven young Guardsmen from the 2nd Battalion, 108th Infantry Division of the New York Army National Guard and focused heavily on the stresses associated with Guardsmen being called to combat service. Of course, these stories are important, and an analysis of resiliency should by no means detract from the reality of pain and suffering caused by war; however, this chapter helps bring to light the need to understand under what conditions citizen-soldiers show resiliency despite multiple deployments.

2. To put this into Zurcher's conceptualization, during deployments, these reservists move from seeing their soldier role as ephemeral to seeing it as of a master status. See Louis A. Zurcher Jr., "The Naval Reservist: An Empirical Assessment of Ephemeral Role Enactment," *Social Forces* 53 (1977): 753–68.

3. The key here for prior active-duty soldiers was that their service had involved at least one deployment. Those who had transferred into the reserve system following active-duty service spent within the contiguous United States were more likely to have encountered struggles during their deployments to Ft. McHenry and Iraq. While studies on reservists' ability to handle deployments based on prior active-duty deployments experience are absent from the research literature, a body of literature examines the effects of prior combat experience on the psychological well-being of active-duty soldiers as they reenter combat zones. For a review of this literature and results of the most recent work on Iraqi war combat-zone veterans, see William D. S. Killgore, Melba C. Stetz, Carl A. Castro, and Charles W. Hoge, "The Effects of Prior Combat Experience on the Expression of Somatic and Affective Symptoms in Deploying Soldiers," *Journal of Psychosomatic Research* 60 (2006): 379–85.

4. All of the soldiers wanted to be proud of the work they had done through their deployments, but for many who are addressed in chapter 5, individual politics or lack of home front support tended to impede their ability to express strong

pride in their work. Alternatively, they may express pride in having served in a conflict they did not personally believe to be just or having survived the perceived disruptions to their civilian lives.

5. The entire literature in the field of on emotional stressors of war is too vast to note here, but more recent articles and books include Matthew J. Friedman, "Posttraumatic Stress Disorder among Military Returnees from Afghanistan and Iraq," *American Journal of Psychiatry* 163 (2006): 586–93; Bruce P. Dohrenwend, J. Blake Turner, Nicholas A. Turse, Ben G. Adams, Karestan C. Koenen, and Randall Marshall, "The Psychological Risks of Vietnam for U.S. Veterans: A Revisit with New Data and Methods," *Science* 313 (2006): 979–82; Charles W. Hoge, Carl A. Castro, Stephen C. Messer, Dennis McGurk, Dave I. Cotting, and Robert L. Koffman, "Combat Duty in Iraq and Afghanistan, Mental Health Problems, and Barriers to Care," *New England Journal of Medicine* 351 (2004): 13–22; Ford et al., "Psychosocial Debriefing after Operation Desert Storm"; Charles C. Hendrix, Marjorie A. Erdmann, and Kathleen Briggs, "Impact of Vietnam Veterans' Arousal and Avoidance on Spouses' Perception of Family Life," *American Journal of Family Therapy* 26 (1998): 115–28; Lisa Teague Caselli and Robert W. Motta, "The Effect of PTSD and Combat Level on Vietnam Veterans' Perceptions of Child Behavior and Marital Adjustment," *Journal of Clinical Psychology* 51 (1995): 4–13; Charles R. Figley, "Coping with Stressors on the Home Front," *Journal of Social Issues* 49 (1993): 51–72; Eric G. Benotsch, Kevin Brailey, Jennifer J. Vasterling, Madeline Uddo, Joseph I. Constans, and Patricia B. Sutker, "War Zone Stress, Personal and Environmental Resources, and PTSD Symptoms in Gulf War Veterans: A Longitudinal Perspective," *Journal of Abnormal Psychology* 109 (2000): 205–13; D. Michael Glenn, Jean C. Beckham, Michelle E. Feldman, Angela C. Kirby, Michael A. Hertzberg, and Scott D. Moore, "Violence and Hostility among Families of Vietnam Veterans with Combat-Related Posttraumatic Stress Disorder," *Violence and Victims* 17 (2002): 473–89; John A. Stuart and Paul D. Bliese, "The Long-Term Effects of Operation Desert Storm on the Psychological Distress of U.S. Army Reserve and National Guard Veterans," *Journal of Applied Social Psychology* 28 (1998): 1–22; Zahava Solomon, "The Effect of Combat-Related Posttraumatic Stress Disorder on the Family," *Psychiatry* 51 (1988): 323–29; Robert J. Ursano and Ann E. Norwood, eds., *Emotional Aftermath of the Persian Gulf War* (Washington, DC: American Psychiatric Press, 1996).

6. In the recent RAND Corporation study, focus group participants—all active-duty personnel—returning from Iraq and Afghanistan deployments report both negative and positive aspects of their deployments. Many participants reported deployment-related stresses, including fast-paced work away from family and friends, increased frequency and length of deployments, long work hours, uncertainty of deployment dates and return dates, and reintegration adjustments with family after returning home. While these are familiar themes, the report also explores several benefits that the servicemen and -women report from their deployments. Among the positive aspects, focus group participants reported satisfaction with increasing military pay, having an opportunity to put training and preparation to work in real-world situations, increasing responsibility, gaining a sense of accomplishment in having contributed to a larger cause, and increasing

bonds with unit members. See Hosek, Kavanagh, and Miller, *How Deployments Affect Service Members,* 50–53.

7. U.S. military wounded and casualty figures from *Washington Post,* "Faces of the Fallen," http://projects.washingtonpost.com/fallen/page1/ (accessed July 30, 2007); U.S. wounded figures from the Department of Defense, "Operation Iraqi Freedom (OIF) U.S. Casualty Status" and "Operation Enduring Freedom (OEF) U.S. Casualty Status," http://www.defenselink.mil/news/casualty.pdf (accessed July 30, 2007); Iraqi death count from Steven R. Hurst, "Iraqi Official: 150,000 Civilians Dead," *Washington Post,* November 10, 2006, http://www.washingtonpost.com/wp-dyn/content/article/2006/11/10/AR2006111000164.html (accessed December 21, 2006).

8. For Colonel Hoge's testimony, see U.S. Congress, House of Representatives, Committee on Veterans' Affairs, *Hearing on Post Traumatic Stress Disorder and Traumatic Brain Injury,* 109th Cong., 2nd sess., September 28, 2006, http://www.house.gov/va/hearings/schedule109/sep06/9-28-06/CharlesHoge.pdf (accessed November 16, 2006). In early May 2007, the Defense Department released the findings of its most recent mental health assessment, the fourth Mental Health Advisory Team survey (MHAT IV), which indicated that extended deployments, multiple deployments, and limited time home between deployments were increasing soldiers' mental stress experiences; see Sara Wood, "Defense Department Releases Finding of Mental Health Assessment," *American Forces Press Service,* May 4, 2007, http://www.defenselink.mil/news/newsarticle aspx?id= 33055 (accessed May 5, 2007). In the summer of 2007 the Department of Defense Task Force on Mental Health released a report indicating that 38 percent of soldiers and 31 percent of marines report some degree of "psychological symptoms" and that within the National Guard the figures rise to 49 percent of returning soldiers. Psychological symptoms are highest among those soldiers with repeat deployments. See *An Achievable Vision: Report of the Department of Defense Task Force on Mental Health* (Falls Church, VA: Defense Health Board).

9. Examples of feature news stories, while too numerous to receive a full account here, include Anderson, "Bringing It All Back Home"; Benedict Carey, "The Struggle to Gauge a War's Psychological Cost," *New York Times,* November 26, 2005, A1.

Chapter Five

1. Quoted in John F. Marszalek, *Sherman: A Soldier's Passion for Order* (New York: Free Press, 1993), 477.

2. See Arlie Russell Hochschild, *The Time Bind: When Work Becomes Home and Home Becomes Work* (New York: Metropolitan, 1997), 205.

3. For analysis on family conflict and military retention following Operation Desert Storm, see Leora N. Rosen and Doris Briley Durand, "The Family Factor and Retention among Married Soldiers Deployed in Operation Desert Storm," *Military Psychology* 7 (1995): 221–34.

4. For the rush to the altar among soldiers called to duty during World War II, see Steven Mintz and Susan Kellogg, *Domestic Revolutions: A Social History of American Family Life* (New York: Random House, 1988), 151–54.

5. Leo Tolstoy, *Anna Karenina* (1875; New York: Random House, 2000), 3.

6. David R. Segal and Mady Wechsler Segal, *Pathway to the Future: A Review of Military Family Research* (Scranton, PA: Marywood University, 1999).

7. See for example, Jo Knox and David H. Price, "Total Force and the New American Military Family: Implications for Social Work Practice," *Families in Society* 80 (1999): 128–37; James A. Martin, Leora N. Rosen, and Linette R. Sparacino, eds., *The Military Family: A Practice Guide for Human Services Providers* (Westport, CT: Praeger, 2000); David E. Rohall, Mady Wechsler Segal, and David R. Segal, "Examining the Importance of Organizational Supports on Family Adjustment to Army Life in a Period of Increasing Separation," *Journal of Political and Military Sociology* 27 (1999): 49–65; Mady Wechsler Segal, "The Military and the Family as Greedy Institutions," *Armed Forces and Society* 13 (1986): 9–38; Jay Stanley, Mady Wechsler Segal, and Charlotte Jeanne Laughton, "Grass Roots Family Action and Military Policy Responses," *Marriage and Family Review* 15 (1990): 207–33.

8. Margaret Harrell provides a voice for active-duty army wives of low-ranking soldiers in *Invisible Women: Junior Enlisted Army Wives* (Santa Monica, CA: RAND, 2000).

9. A full three years later, the Department of Defense Task Force on Mental Health acknowledged serious shortcomings in the military's ability to address the mental health problems of soldiers, including the dissemination of information regarding resources for soldiers in need. See Department of Defense Task Force on Mental Health, *An Achievable Vision: Report of the Department of Defense Task Force on Mental Health* (Falls Church, VA: Defense Health Board, 2007).

10. A voluntary family support network was available to the families of the 893rd, although this network received mixed reviews from company members. For those who were geographically close and got along well with the company wives who ran the support network, the praise runs high. Enlisted reservist Adam Reed even credits the family support network with saving his marriage. Others who felt left out of the loop or who were geographically so far-flung from the reserve center that contact other than e-mail was relatively impractical had less praise for the network.

Chapter Six

1. Thom Shanker and Michael R. Gordon, "Top Commanders Appear Set to Urge Larger U.S. Military," *New York Times,* December 15, 2006, A16.

2. Commission on the National Guard and Reserves, *Hearing on Proposed Changes to National Guard,* panel 2, December 14, 2006, http://www.cngr.gov/hearing121314/1214cngr-panel2.pdf (accessed April 2, 2007), 2.

3. Thom Shanker and Jim Rutenberg, "President Wants to Increase Size of Armed Forces," *New York Times,* December 20, 2006, A1.

4. David S. Cloud, "Military Eases Its Rules for Mobilizing Reserves," *New York Times,* January 12, 2007, A13.

5. Commission on the National Guard and Reserves, *Hearing on Proposed Changes to National Guard,* panel 2, December 14, 2006, http://www.cngr.gov/hearing121314/1214cngr-panel2.pdf (accessed April 2, 2007).

6. Several cases of reserve soldiers' refusal to redeploy are making their way through the legal system; see Monica Davey, "Eight Soldiers Plan to Sue over Army Tours of Duty," *New York Times,* December 6, 2004, A15; Dean E. Murphy, "Soldier Sues over Tour Made Longer," *New York Times,* August 18, 2004, A20.

7. Refusal to comply with drill duties has some history within the reserves. Shelley Perry, James Griffith, and Terry White reported in 1991 that the Army Reserve lost about 30 percent of its members annually and that the majority of this attrition occurred among junior enlisted members who simply stopped fulfilling their weekend drill obligations and were subsequently transferred to the Army Individual Ready Reserve as "unsatisfactory participants" (Shelley Perry, James Griffith, and Terry White, "Retention of Junior Enlisted Soldiers in the All-Volunteer Army Reserve," *Armed Forces and Society* 18 [1991]: 111–33).

8. We attempted to contact discharged and absent men and women, but not a single one responded to our efforts.

9. Following the first Gulf War, the Army Reserve experienced an initial downturn in the number of college students among its new recruits; see James Griffith and Shelley Perry, "Wanting to Soldier: Enlistment Motivations of Army Reserve Recruits before and after Operation Desert Storm," *Military Psychology* 5 (1993): 127–39.

10. Thom Shanker and Michael R. Gordon, "Strained, Army Looks to Guard for More Relief," *New York Times,* September 22, 2006, A1; Ann Scott Tyson, "Possible Iraq Deployments Would Stretch Reserve Force; Leaders Express Concern over Troop Rotation Plans," *Washington Post,* November 5, 2006, A01.

11. Oren Dorell, "Iraq War about to Equal Time U.S. Spent Fighting WWII," *USA Today,* November 24, 2006, 1; "The War in Iraq and World War II Have Now Both Lasted Three Years, Eight Months, and Seven Days," *Washington Post,* November 26, 2006, B04.

12. Evan M. Wooten, "Banging on the Backdraft Door: The Constitutional Validity of Stop-Loss in the Military," *William and Mary Law Review* 47 (2005): 1063. This sense of conscription is not without official objection on the part of some reserve component soldiers. Eight members of the Arkansas National Guard and a member of the California National Guard have filed separate suits against the army, challenging the stop-loss policy.

13. Reservists' objections to being mobilized are certainly not unique to the current conflicts in Afghanistan and Iraq. Throughout the twentieth century, reservists and those close to them have objected when called to increased duty. Prior to the attack on Pearl Harbor, reserve troops had already been mobilized for a year and were growing weary of their extended service. The Japanese attack put a general end to the low reserve morale, but it surfaced again as many reserve veterans of World War II were called again for service during the Korean War. The Berlin crisis of 1961 also met resistance from reservists. See Martin Binkin and William W. Kaufmann, *U.S. Army Guard and Reserve: Rhetoric, Realities, Risks* (Washington, DC: Brookings Institution, 1989); Richard B. Crossland and James T. Currie, *Twice the Citizen: A History of the United States Army Reserve, 1908–1983* (Washington, DC: Office of the Chief, Army Reserve, 1984).

14. One way in which the army has met its recruiting goals between 2003 and

2006 is to increase the number of waivers granted to new recruits with criminal backgrounds by 65 percent; see Lizette Alvarez, "Army Giving More Waivers in Recruiting," *New York Times,* February 14, 2007, A1.

15. Universal service is not typically universal to the whole of the citizenship but to some specific age group of able-bodied individuals and is more typically a service of men than women; see John Whiteclay Chambers II, *To Raise an Army: The Draft Comes to Modern America* (New York: Free Press, 1987).

16. John C. Fitzpatrick, ed., *The Writings of George Washington* (Washington, DC: U.S. Government Printing Office, 1938), 26:389.

17. David R. Segal, *Recruiting for Uncle Sam: Citizenship and Military Manpower Policy* (Lawrence: University Press of Kansas, 1989), 20.

18. While the War of 1812, the Indian wars, and the Mexican War were fought primarily through a volunteer militia system, both the Union and Confederate Armies raised troops through systems of conscription that heavily favored exemption of the rich. The first national registration for selective service took place in 1917 in preparation for World War I, but between 1919 and 1940, the United States reverted back to an all-volunteer military. Following World War II, President Harry S. Truman fought unsuccessfully with Congress to establish universal military training of all young men. The members of the Gates Commission were divided on the feasibility of developing an all-volunteer force. Although the commission was charged with developing "a comprehensive plan for eliminating conscription," retired generals Alfred Gruenther and Lauris Norstad—both former supreme allied commanders in Europe—remained skeptical of the idea of an all-volunteer force. Despite having an all-volunteer force established by the mid-1970s, President Gerald Ford reinstated a peacetime registration to maintain the option of having a "deep stand-by." President Jimmy Carter's efforts to reinstate draft registration followed. Although Ronald Reagan criticized this policy during his first presidential campaign efforts, he soon supported the current law requiring young men to register within thirty days of their eighteenth birthdays. See David R. Segal, *Recruiting for Uncle Sam;* Chambers, *To Raise an Army.*

19. U.S. Congress, Senate, Committee on Armed Services, *Nomination of John D. Lavelle, General Creighton W. Abrams, and Admiral John S. McCain,* 92nd Cong., 2nd sess. (Washington, DC: U.S. Government Printing Office, 1972), 140–41.

20. Binkin and Kaufmann, *U.S. Army Guard and Reserve,* 2.

21. James R. Helmly, "A Streamlined Army Reserve," *Washington Post,* September 22, 2003, 23.

22. Morris Janowitz, "Volunteer Armed Forces and Military Purpose," *Foreign Affairs* 50 (1972): 427–43; Morris Janowitz, "Toward an All-Volunteer Military," *Public Interest* 27 (1972): 104–17; Morris Janowitz, "The All-Volunteer Military as a 'Sociopolitical' Problem," *Social Problems* 22 (1975): 432–49. See also Thomas E. Ricks, "The Widening Gap between the Military and Society," *Atlantic Monthly,* July 1997, 67–78; David E. Rohall, Morten G. Ender, and Michael D. Matthews, "The Effects of Military Affiliation, Gender, and Political Ideology on Attitudes toward the Wars in Afghanistan and Iraq," *Armed Forces and Society* 33 (2006): 59–77.

Appendix A

1. By our own count using LexisNexis, the yearly referencing of *citizen-soldiers* was virtually absent from news transcripts from the end of the Vietnam War through the early 1990s. It begins to be referenced with some frequency, averaging thirty times per year, during the period following the first Gulf War through the 1990s. Then, beginning in 2001, *citizen-soldiers* appears on average two hundred times yearly through 2006.

2. In military sociology, *citizen-soldier* is an unsettled concept. Some—for example, Gary Hart, *The Minuteman: Restoring an Army of the People* (New York: Free Press, 1998)—have associated citizen-soldiers entirely with the minutemen of the Revolutionary War even though minutemen were an elite group of the militias, similar to what we now have as combat-ready reserve units; see John R. Galvin, *The Minute Men: A Compact History of the Defenders of the American Colonies* (New York: Hawthorn, 1967). Those designated as citizen-soldiers in World War II were those drafted into combat, whereas that designation did not stick during the Vietnam War; see Charles Moskos, *A Call to Civic Service: National Service for Country and Community* (New York: Free Press, 1988), 21–24. Moskos, a leading authority on the topic, has called for a broadened notion of citizen-soldier to include all who would engage in compulsory national service, "serving societal needs, military and civilian, that neither the market nor conventional governmental bureaucracies can meet" (40). For those who stick to the idea of citizen-soldiers as military personnel, the true citizen-soldier is defined as those who serve a pressing governmental cause as an obligation or through state imposition, who are part of a military whose composition is representative of the state, and whose "identity is overwhelmingly civilian" (Eliot Cohen, "Twilight of the Citizen-Soldier," *Parameters: U.S. Army War College Quarterly* 31 [2001]: 5).

3. For us, group belonging includes those subject positions we are thrown into or where membership is nearly automatic, as in the case of gender groupings and generational groupings, such as teens or elderly; see Iris Marion Young, *Justice and the Politics of Difference* (Princeton: Princeton University Press, 1990). We also include associational memberships, or groups in which we have considerable say about whether we affiliate, including the identities associated with work and occupations; see Michael Walzer, *Spheres of Justice* (New York: Basic Books, 1983). Critical events that shape our identities include illnesses and diseases, accidents, and in the case of reservists, the interruption brought on by involuntary deployments. On the issue of how events shape identities, see Michael Musheno, "Legal Consciousness on the Margins of Society: Struggles against Stigmatization in the AIDS Crisis," *Identities: Global Studies in Culture and Power* 2 (1995): 101–27. On the significance of place in shaping identities, see Lisa Sanchez, "Enclosure Acts and Exclusionary Practices: Neighborhood Associations, Community Police, and the Expulsion of the Sexual Outlaw," in *Between Law and Culture: Relocating Legal Studies,* edited by David Theo Goldberg, Michael Musheno, and Lisa C. Bower (Minneapolis: University of Minnesota Press, 2001), 122–41; Steven Maynard-Moody and Michael Musheno,

Cops, Teachers, Counselors: Stories from the Front Lines of Public Service (Ann Arbor: University of Michigan Press, 2003), 51. Most subject positions we occupy have been sociopolitically filled with cultural meaning, including those associated with race and ethnicity, gender and sexuality; see David Theo Goldberg, "States of Whiteness," in *Between Law and Culture: Relocating Legal Studies*, edited by David Theo Goldberg, Michael Musheno, and Lisa Bower (Minneapolis: University of Minnesota Press, 2001), 174–94. On the multiple subject positions we occupy, see Kimberly Crenshaw, "Mapping the Margins: Intersectionality, Identity Politics, and Violence against Women of Color," in *After Identity*, edited by Dan Danielsen and Karen Engle (New York: Routledge, 1994), 93–114. On how we compose our own identities, see Trish Oberweis and Michael Musheno, *Knowing Rights: State Actors' Stories of Power, Identity, and Morality* (Burlington, VT: Ashgate/Dartmouth, 2001), 56–58.

4. Our interviews were framed primarily within the reservists' relationships to family, military, and civilian work or education. We recognized that this approach downplayed their roles in other institutions such as religion, medicine, sports, law, and politics except where these areas intersect within civilian work, such as being a minister or corrections officer.

5. See especially Mady Wechsler Segal, "The Military and the Family as Greedy Institutions," *Armed Forces and Society* 13 (1986): 9–38. Segal draws on Lewis Coser's original conceptualization of "greedy institutions" that "seek exclusive and undivided loyalty and . . . attempt to reduce the claims of competing roles and status positions on those they wish to encompass within their boundaries. Their demands on the person are omnivorous. . . . Greedy institutions are characterized by the fact that they exercise pressures on component individuals to weaken their ties, or not to form any ties, with other institutions or persons that might make claims that conflict with their own demands" (Lewis A. Coser, *Greedy Institutions: Patterns of Undivided Commitment* [New York: Free Press, 1974], 4–6). While Coser originally theorized that family is a greedier institution for traditional housewives than for men, changes within the family over the more than three decades since the publication of *Greedy Institutions* would suggest that the demands on men's commitment to family have increased.

6. For a recent argument regarding the extension of mass-media-embedded war reporting to the application of military families as a greedy institution, see Morten G. Ender, Kathleen M. Campbell, Toya J. Davis, and Patrick R. Michaelis, "Greedy Media: Army Families, Embedded Reporting, and War in Iraq," *Sociological Focus* 40 (2007): 48–71.

7. See especially the emerging work by Ryan Kelty, Todd Woodruff, and David R. Segal, "Relative Salience of Family versus Soldier Role Identity," paper presented at the meeting of the International Sociological Association, Durban, South Africa, 2006.

8. Gary L. Bowen and Dennis K. Orthner, eds. *The Organization Family: Work and Family Linkages in the U.S. Military* (Westport, CT: Praeger, 1989); James A Martin, Leora N. Rosen, and Linette R. Sparacino, eds., *The Military Family: A Practice Guide for Human Service Providers* (Westport, CT: Praeger, 2000); Walter Schumm, D. Bruce Bell, and Giao Tran, *Family Adaptation to the*

Demands of Army Life: A Review of Findings (Alexandria, VA: U.S. Army Research Institute for the Behavioral and Social Sciences, 1994).

9. While we give substantial attention to the grip of institutional spheres on the reservists' lives, we also kept an eye out for instances of individual and group "agency," or reservists' ability to reconstitute these spheres, leaving their own marks on them, through their capacities to initiate and resist. Thus, our frame of inquiry rejects the idea that social structure is a straightjacket. For an example of another contemporary work along these lines, see John Gilliom, *Overseers of the Poor: Surveillance, Resistance, and the Limits of Privacy* (Chicago: University of Chicago Press, 2001).

10. Tracy Kidder, *My Detachment: A Memoir* (New York: Random House, 2006), 6.

11. Factually, for every 1,000 military personnel deployed to Iraq and the Gulf region, approximately 230 solders are combat troops. See Thom Shanker, "Pulling Out Combat Troops Would Still Leave Most Forces in Iraq," *New York Times,* December 10, 2006, 18.

12. Both of us are question-driven in our research endeavors. We see interpretative scholarship as a logic of inquiry, and at the same time, we feel strongly that the substantive grounds of a particular project also define the inquiry one undertakes. For this pragmatic or "practice-centered view" of interpretative inquiry, see Joe Soss, "Talking Our Way to Meaningful Explanations: A Practice-Centered View of Interviewing for Interpretative Inquiry," in *Interpretation and Method: Empirical Research Methods and the Interpretive Turn,* edited by Dvora Yanow and Peregrine Schwartz-Shea (London: Sharpe, 2006), 127–50. For a more doctrinal view of interpretive research that focuses on a paradigm of interpretivism, see Dvora Yanow, "Neither Rigorous or Objective? Interrogating Criteria for Knowledge Claims in Interpretive Science, in *Interpretation and Method: Empirical Research Methods and the Interpretive Turn,* edited by Dvora Yanow and Peregrine Schwartz-Shea (London: Sharpe, 2006), 67–88.

13. Joe Soss, *Unwanted Claims: The Politics of Participation in the U.S. Welfare System* (Ann Arbor: University of Michigan Press, 2000).

14. Gilliom, *Overseers of the Poor.*

15. Soss, "Talking our Way to Meaningful Explanations," 140.

16. Maynard-Moody and Musheno, *Cops, Teachers, Counselors.*

17. For the craft of engaging in these later stages of interpretation that produce an interpretive book, see Steven Maynard-Moody and Michael Musheno, "Stories for Research," in *Interpretation and Method: Empirical Research Methods and the Interpretive Turn,* edited by Dvora Yanow and Peregrine Schwartz-Shea (London: Sharpe, 2006), 316–31.

References

Alvarez, Lizette. "Army Giving More Waivers in Recruiting." *New York Times,* February 14, 2007, A1.

Alvarez, Lizette, and Andrew Lehren. "Another Grim Milestone for U.S." *New York Times,* January 1, 2007, A1, A9.

Ambrose, Stephen E. *Band of Brothers: E Company, 506th Regiment, 101st Airborne from Normandy to Hitler's Eagle's Nest.* New York: Simon and Schuster, 2001.

Anderson, Scott. "Bringing It All Back Home." *New York Times Magazine,* May 28, 2006, 36–43, 56, 63.

Arkes, Jeremy, and M. Rebecca Kilburn. *Modeling Reserve Recruiting: Estimates of Enlistments.* Santa Monica, CA: RAND, 2005.

Bacevich, Andrew J. *The New American Militarism: How Americans Are Seduced by War.* New York: Oxford University Press, 2005.

Baskir, Lawrence M., and William A. Strauss. *Chance and Circumstance: The Draft, the War, and the Vietnam Generation.* New York: Knopf, 1978.

Benotsch, Eric G., Kevin Brailey, Jennifer J. Vasterling, Madeline Uddo, Joseph I. Constans, and Patricia B. Sutker. "War Zone Stress, Personal and Environmental Resources, and PTSD Symptoms in Gulf War Veterans: A Longitudinal Perspective." *Journal of Abnormal Psychology* 109 (2000): 205–13.

Berman, Larry. *Planning a Tragedy: The Americanization of the War in Vietnam.* New York: Norton, 1982.

Binkin, Martin. *Who Will Fight the Next War? The Changing Face of the American Military.* Washington, DC: Brookings Institution, 1993.

Binkin, Martin, and William W. Kaufmann. *U.S. Army Guard and Reserve: Rhetoric, Realities, Risks.* Washington, DC: Brookings Institution, 1989.

Bowen, Gary L., and Dennis K. Orthner, eds. *The Organization Family: Work and Family Linkages in the U.S. Military.* Westport, CT: Praeger, 1989.

Brinkerhoff, John R., Ted Silva, and John Seitz. *United States Army Reserve in Operation Desert Storm, Enemy Prisoner of War Operations: The 800th Military Police Brigade.* Washington, DC: Chief, U.S. Army Reserve, 1992.

Brokaw, Tom. "To War and Back." Special Report, NBC, December 18, 2005. http:www.msnbc.com/id/10402820/

Buzzell, Colby. *My War: Killing Time in Iraq.* New York: Putnam Adult, 2005.

Carafano, James Jay. "The Army Reserves and the Abrams Doctrine: Unfulfilled Promise, Uncertain Future." Heritage Foundation Lecture 869. Paper presented at the Foreign Policy Research Institute conference on the future of the reserves and National Guard, Philadelphia, April 18, 2005. http://www.heritage.org/Research/National Security/hl869.cfm. Accessed July 27, 2007.

Carey, Benedict. 2005. "The Struggle to Gauge a War's Psychological Cost." *New York Times,* November 26, 2005, A1.

Caselli, Lisa Teague, and Robert W. Motta. "The Effect of PTSD and Combat Level on Vietnam Veterans' Perceptions of Child Behavior and Marital Adjustment." *Journal of Clinical Psychology* 51 (1995): 4–13.

Chambers, John Whiteclay, II. *To Raise an Army: The Draft Comes to Modern America.* New York: Free Press, 1987.

Cloud, David S. "Military Eases Its Rules for Mobilizing Reserves." *New York Times,* January 12, 2007, A13.

CNN. "More National Guard Units May Get Second Tours in Iraq." November 11, 2006, http://www.cnn.com/2006/US/11/11/iraq.national.guard.ap/index.html. Accessed November 11, 2006.

Cohen, Eliot A. "Twilight of the Citizen-Soldier." *Parameters: U.S. Army War College Quarterly* 31 (2001): 23–28.

Commission on the National Guard and Reserves. *Hearing on Proposed Changes to National Guard.* Panel 2, December 14, 2006. http://www.cngr.gov/hearing121314/1214cngr-panel2.pdf. Accessed April 2, 2007.

Corbett, Sara. "The Women's War." *New York Times Magazine,* March 18, 2007, 42.

Coser, Lewis A. *Greedy Institutions: Patterns of Undivided Commitment.* New York: Free Press, 1974.

Crawford, John. *The Last True Story I'll Ever Tell: An Accidental Soldier's Account of the War in Iraq.* New York: Riverhead, 2005.

Crenshaw, Kimberly. "Mapping the Margins: Intersectionality, Identity Politics, and Violence against Women of Color." In *After Identity,* edited by Dan Danielsen and Karen Engle, 93–114. New York: Routledge, 1994.

Crossland, Richard B., and James T. Currie. *Twice the Citizen: A History of the United States Army Reserve, 1908–1983.* Washington, DC: Office of the Chief, Army Reserve, 1984.

Davey, Monica. "Eight Soldiers Plan to Sue over Army Tours of Duty." *New York Times,* December 6, 2004, A15.

Dohrenwend, Bruce P., J. Blake Turner, Nicholas A. Turse, Ben G. Adams, Karestan C. Koenen, and Randall Marshall. "The Psychological Risks of

Vietnam for U.S. Veterans: A Revisit with New Data and Methods." *Science* 313 (2006): 979–82.

Dorell, Oren. "Iraq War about to Equal Time U.S. Spent Fighting WWII." *USA Today*, November 24, 2006, 1.

Duncan, Stephen M. *Citizen Warriors: America's National Guard and Reserve Forces and the Politics of National Security.* Novato, CA: Presidio, 1996.

Ender, Morten G., ed. *Military Brats and Other Global Nomads: Growing Up in Organization Families.* Westport, CT: Praeger, 2002.

Ender, Morten G., Kathleen M. Campbell, Toya J. Davis, and Patrick R. Michaelis. "Greedy Media: Army Families, Embedded Reporting, and War in Iraq." *Sociological Focus* 40 (2007): 48–71.

Figley, Charles R. "Coping with Stressors on the Home Front." *Journal of Social Issues* 49 (1993): 51–72.

Fitzpatrick, John C., ed. *The Writings of George Washington.* Vol. 26. Washington, DC: U.S. Government Printing Office, 1938.

Ford, Julian D., Patricia Chandler, Barbara Thacker, David Greaves, David Shaw, Shirley Sennhauser, and Lawrence Schwartz. "Family Systems Therapy after Operation Desert Storm with European-Theater Veterans." *Journal of Marital and Family Therapy* 24 (1998): 243–51.

Ford, Julian D., David Shaw, Shirley Sennhauser, David Greaves, Barbara Thacker, Patricia Chandler, Lawrence Schwartz, and Valerie McClain. "Psychosocial Debriefing after Operation Desert Storm: Marital and Family Assessment and Intervention." *Journal of Social Issues* 49 (1993): 73–103.

Friedman, Matthew J. "Posttraumatic Stress Disorder among Military Returnees from Afghanistan and Iraq." *American Journal of Psychiatry* 163 (2006): 586–93.

Galvin, John R. *The Minute Men: A Compact History of the Defenders of the American Colonies.* New York: Hawthorn, 1967.

Garey, Anita Ilta. *Weaving Work and Motherhood.* Philadelphia: Temple University Press, 1999.

Gebhardt, James F. "The Road to Abu Ghraib: U.S. Army Detainee Doctrine and Experience." *Military Review* 85 (2005): 44–50.

Getler, Michael. "Make-Believe Mobilization Showed Major Flaws." *Washington Post*, July 14, 1980, A6.

Gilliom, John. *Overseers of the Poor: Surveillance, Resistance, and the Limits of Privacy.* Chicago: University of Chicago Press, 2001.

Glenn, D. Michael, Jean C. Beckham, Michelle E. Feldman, Angela C. Kirby, Michael A. Hertzberg, and Scott D. Moore. "Violence and Hostility among Families of Vietnam Veterans with Combat-Related Posttraumatic Stress Disorder." *Violence and Victims* 17 (2002): 473–90.

Goldberg, David Theo. "States of Whiteness." In *Between Law and Culture: Relocating Legal Studies*, edited by David Theo Goldberg, Michael Musheno, and Lisa C. Bower, 174–94. Minneapolis: University of Minnesota Press, 2001.

Griffith, James, and Shelley Perry. "Wanting to Soldier: Enlistment Motivations of Army Reserve Recruits before and after Operation Desert Storm." *Military Psychology* 5 (1993): 127–39.

Groves, John R. *Crossroads in U.S. Military Capability: The 21st Century U.S. Army and the Abrams Doctrine.* Land Warfare Papers 37. Arlington, VA: Institute of Land Warfare, 2001.

Halberstam, David. *The Best and the Brightest.* New York: Random House, 1972.

Hardcastle, Nate, and Clint Willis, eds. *American Soldier: Stories of Special Forces from Iraq to Afghanistan.* New York: Thunder's Mouth, 2002.

Harrell, Margaret C. *Invisible Women: Junior Enlisted Army Wives.* Santa Monica, CA: RAND, 2000.

Hart, Gary. *The Minuteman: Restoring an Army of the People.* New York: Free Press, 1998.

Helmly, James R. "A Streamlined Army Reserve." *Washington Post,* September 22, 2003, 23.

Hendrix, Charles C., Marjorie A. Erdmann, and Kathleen Briggs. "Impact of Vietnam Veterans' Arousal and Avoidance on Spouses' Perceptions of Family Life." *American Journal of Family Therapy* 26 (1998): 115–29.

Hickman, Matthew J. "Impact of the Military Reserve Activation on Police Staffing." *Police Chief* 73 (2006). http://policechiefmagazine.org/magazine/index.cfm?fuseaction=archivecontents&issue_id=102006. Accessed May 2, 2007.

Hochschild, Arlie Russell. *The Time Bind: When Work Becomes Home and Home Becomes Work.* New York: Metropolitan, 1997.

Hoge, Charles W., Carl A. Castro, Stephen C. Messer, Dennis McGurk, Dave I. Cotting, and Robert L. Koffman. "Combat Duty in Iraq and Afghanistan, Mental Health Problems, and Barriers to Care." *New England Journal of Medicine* 351 (2004): 13–22.

Hosek, James, Jennifer Kavanagh, and Laura Miller. *How Deployments Affect Service Members.* Santa Monica, CA: RAND, 2006.

Hurst, Steven R. "Iraqi Official: 150,000 Civilians Dead." *Washington Post,* November 10, 2006. http://www.washingtonpost.com/wp-dyn/content/article/2006/11/10/AR2006111000164.html. Accessed December 21, 2006.

Janowitz, Morris. "The All-Volunteer Military as a 'Sociopolitical' Problem." *Social Problems* 22 (1975): 432–49.

Janowitz, Morris. "Toward an All-Volunteer Military." *Public Interest* 27 (1972): 104–17.

Janowitz, Morris. "Volunteer Armed Forces and Military Purpose." *Foreign Affairs* 50 (1972): 427–43.

Johnson, Lyndon Baines. *Vantage Point: Perspectives of the Presidency, 1963–1969.* New York: Holt, Rinehart, and Winston, 1971.

Kapp, Lawrence. *Operations Noble Eagle, Enduring Freedom, and Iraqi Freedom: Questions and Answers about U.S. Military Personnel, Compensation, and Force Structure.* Congressional Research Service Report for Congress, February 16, 2005. http://fas.org/sgp/crs/natsec/RL31334.pdf. Accessed April 29, 2007.

Kelty, Ryan, Todd Woodruff, and David R. Segal. "Relative Salience of Family versus Soldier Role Identity." Paper presented at the meeting of the International Sociological Association, Durban, South Africa, July 24, 2006.

Kidder, Tracy. *My Detachment: A Memoir.* New York: Random House, 2006.

Killgore, William D. S., Melba C. Stetz, Carl A. Castro, and Charles W. Hoge. "The Effects of Prior Combat Experience on the Expression of Somatic and Affective Symptoms in Deploying Soldiers." *Journal of Psychosomatic Research* 60 (2006): 379–85.

Kirby, Sheila Nataraj. "The Impact of Deployment on the Retention of Military Reservists." *Armed Forces and Society* 26 (2000): 259–84.

Kirby, Sheila Nataraj, and Scott Naftel. *The Effects of Mobilization on Retention of Enlisted Reservists after Operation Desert Shield/Storm.* Santa Monica, CA: RAND, 1998.

Knox, Jo, and David H. Price. "Total Force and the New American Military Family: Implications for Social Work Practice." *Families in Society* 80 (1999): 128–37.

Lembcke, Jerry. *The Spitting Image: Myth, Memory, and the Legacy of Vietnam.* New York: New York University Press, 1998.

Little, Roger W. "Buddy Relations and Combat Soldier Performance." In *The New Military,* edited by Morris Janowitz, 195–224. New York: Sage, 1964.

MacCoun, Robert, Elizabeth Kier, and Aaron Belkin. "Does Social Cohesion Determine Motivation in Combat? An Old Question with an Old Answer." *Armed Forces and Society* 32 (2005): 1–9.

Marszalek, John F. *Sherman: A Soldier's Passion for Order.* New York: Free Press, 1993.

Martin, James A., Leora N. Rosen, and Linette R. Sparacino, eds. *The Military Family: A Practice Guide for Human Service Providers.* Westport, CT: Praeger, 2000.

Maxfield, Betty D. *Army Profile, FY04.* Washington, DC: Office of Army Demographics, 2004. ww.armyg1.army.mil/hr/demographics/FY04%20Army%20Profile.pdf. Accessed April 10, 2007.

Maynard-Moody, Steven, and Michael Musheno. *Cops, Teachers, Counselors: Stories from the Front Lines of Public Service.* Ann Arbor: University of Michigan Press, 2003.

Maynard-Moody, Steven, and Michael Musheno. "Stories for Research." In *Interpretation and Method: Empirical Research Methods and the Interpretive Turn,* edited by Dvora Yanow and Peregrine Schwartz-Shea, 316–31. London: Sharpe, 2006.

McNamara, Robert S., and Brian VanDeMark. *In Retrospect: The Tragedy and Lessons of Vietnam.* New York: Times Books, 1995.

Mintz, Steven, and Susan Kellogg. *Domestic Revolutions: A Social History of American Family Life.* New York: Random House, 1988.

Moskos, Charles C. *A Call to Civic Service: National Service for Country and Community.* New York: Free Press, 1988.

Moskos, Charles C., and Frank R. Wood, eds. *The Military: More Than Just a Job?* Washington, DC: Pergamon-Brassey's International Defense Publishers, 1988.

Murphy, Dean E. "Soldier Sues over Tour Made Longer." *New York Times,* August 18, 2004, A20.

Musheno, Michael. "Legal Consciousness on the Margins of Society: Struggles against Stigmatization in the AIDS Crisis." *Identities: Global Studies in Culture and Power* 2 (1995): 101–27.

Nuciari, Marina. "Models and Explanations for Military Organization: An Updated Reconsideration." In *Handbook of Sociology of the Military*, edited by Giuseppe Caforio, 61–85. New York: Kluwer Academic/Plenum, 2003.

Oberweis, Trish, and Michael Musheno. *Knowing Rights: State Actors' Stories of Power, Identity, and Morality.* Burlington, VT: Ashgate/Dartmouth, 2001.

Perry, Shelley, James Griffith, and Terry White. "Retention of Junior Enlisted Soldiers in the All-Volunteer Army Reserve." *Armed Forces and Society* 18 (1991): 111–33.

Ricks, Thomas E. "The Widening Gap between the Military and Society." *Atlantic Monthly*, July 1997, 67–78.

Rohall, David E., Morten G. Ender, and Michael D. Matthews. "The Effects of Military Affiliation, Gender, and Political Ideology on Attitudes toward the Wars in Afghanistan and Iraq." *Armed Forces and Society* 33 (2006): 59–77.

Rohall, David E., Mady Wechsler Segal, and David R. Segal. "Examining the Importance of Organizational Supports on Family Adjustments to Army Life in a Period of Increasing Separation." *Journal of Political and Military Sociology* 27 (1999): 49–65.

Rosen, Leora N., and Doris B. Durand. "The Family Factor and Retention among Married Soldiers Deployed in Operation Desert Storm." *Military Psychology* 7 (1995): 221–34.

Rosenbaum, David E. "Kennedy and Hatfield Disagree at Hearing on Volunteer Army." *New York Times*, February 5, 1971, 12.

Sanchez, Lisa. "Enclosure Acts and Exclusionary Practices: Neighborhood Associations, Community Police, and the Expulsion of the Sexual Outlaw." In *Between Law and Culture: Relocating Legal Studies*, edited by David Theo Goldberg, Michael Musheno, and Lisa C. Bower, 122–41. Minneapolis: University of Minnesota Press, 2001.

Schmitt, Eric, and David S. Cloud. "The Reach of War: Troop Deployment; Part-Time Forces on Active Duty Decline Steeply." *New York Times*, July 11, 2005, A1.

Schumm, Walter R., D. Bruce Bell, and Paul A. Gade. "Effects of a Military Overseas Peacekeeping Deployment on Marital Quality, Satisfaction, and Stability." *Psychological Report* 87 (2000): 815–21.

Schumm, Walter R., D. Bruce Bell, and Giao Tran. *Family Adaptation to the Demands of Army Life: A Review of Findings.* Alexandria, VA: U.S. Army Research Institute for the Behavioral and Social Sciences, 1994.

Scott, Wilbur J. *The Politics of Readjustment: Vietnam Veterans since the War.* New York: Aldine de Gruyter, 1993.

Segal, David R. "Measuring the Institutional/Occupational Change Thesis." *Armed Forces and Society* 12 (1986): 351–76.

Segal, David R. *Recruiting for Uncle Sam: Citizenship and Military Manpower Policy.* Lawrence: University Press of Kansas, 1989.

Segal, David R., and Mady Wechsler Segal. *Pathway to the Future: A Review of Military Family Research.* Scranton, PA: Marywood University, 1999.

Segal, Mady Wechsler. "The Military and the Family as Greedy Institutions." *Armed Forces and Society* 13 (1986): 9–38.

Severo, Richard, and Lewis Milford. *The Wages of War: When American Soldiers Came Home from Valley Forge to Vietnam*. New York: Simon and Schuster, 1989.

Shanker, Thom. "Pulling Out Combat Troops Would Still Leave Most Forces in Iraq." *New York Times*, December 10, 2006, 18.

Shanker, Thom, and Michael R. Gordon. "Strained, Army Looks to Guard for More Relief," *New York Times*, September 22, 2006, A1.

Shanker, Thom, and Michael R. Gordon. "Top Commanders Appear Set to Urge Larger U.S. Military." *New York Times*, December 15, 2006, A16.

Shanker, Thom, and Jim Rutenberg. "President Wants to Increase Size of Armed Forces." *New York Times*, December 20, 2006, A1.

Solomon, Zahava. "The Effect of Combat-Related Posttraumatic Stress Disorder on the Family." *Psychiatry* 51 (1988): 323–29.

Sorley, Lewis. "Creighton Abrams and Active-Reserve Integration in Wartime." *Parameters* 21 (1991): 35–50.

Sorley, Lewis. "National Guard and Reserve Forces." In *American Defense Annual, 1991–1992*, edited by Joseph Kruzel, 183–201. New York: Lexington, 1992.

Sorley, Lewis. *Thunderbolt: General Creighton Abrams and the Army of His Times*. New York: Brassey's, 1998.

Soss, Joe. "Talking Our Way to Meaningful Explanations: A Practice-Centered View of Interviewing for Interpretative Inquiry." In *Interpretation and Method: Empirical Research Methods and the Interpretive Turn*, edited by Dvora Yanow and Peregrine Schwartz-Shea, 127–50. London: Sharpe, 2006.

Soss, Joe. *Unwanted Claims: The Politics of Participation in the U.S. Welfare System*. Ann Arbor: University of Michigan Press, 2000.

Stanley, Jay, Mady Wechsler Segal, and Charlotte Jeanne Laughton. "Grass Roots Family Action and Military Policy Responses." *Marriage and Family Review* 15 (1990): 207–33.

Starr, Paul. *The Discarded Army: Veterans after Vietnam*. New York: Charter House, 1973.

Stuart, John A., and Paul D. Bliese. "The Long-Term Effects of Operation Desert Storm on the Psychological Distress of U.S. Army Reserve and National Guard Veterans." *Journal of Applied Social Psychology* 28 (1998): 1–23.

Sweet, Stephen. *College and Society: An Introduction to the Sociological Imagination*. Boston: Allyn and Bacon, 2001.

Taylor, Richard H. *Homeward Bound: American Veterans Return from War*. Westport, CT: Praeger, 2007.

Tolstoy, Leo. *Anna Karenina*. 1875; New York: Random House, 2000.

Tyson, Ann Scott. "Possible Iraq Deployments Would Stretch Reserve Force; Leaders Express Concern over Troop Rotation Plans." *Washington Post*, November 5, 2006, A01.

U.S. Army. "About the Army: Active Duty and Army Reserve." http://www.goarmy.com/about/active_duty_and_reserve.jsp. Accessed May 18, 2006.

U.S. Army. "Army Reserve." http://www.goarmy.com/reserve/nps/index.jsp. Accessed May 18, 2006.

U.S. Congress. House of Representatives. Committee on Veterans' Affairs. *Hearing on Post Traumatic Stress Disorder and Traumatic Brain Injury.* 109th Cong., 2nd sess., September 28, 2006. http://www.house.gov/va/hearings/schedule109/sep06/9–28–06/CharlesHoge.pdf. Accessed November 16, 2006.

U.S. Congress. Senate. Committee on Armed Services. *Nomination of John D. Lavelle, General Creighton W. Abrams, and Admiral John S. McCain.* 92nd Cong., 2nd sess. Washington, DC: U.S. Government Printing Office, 1972.

U.S. Department of Defense. "Operation Iraqi Freedom (OIF) U.S. Casualty Status and Operation Enduring Freedom (OEF) U.S. Casualty Status." http://www.defenselink.mil/news/casualty.pdf. Accessed July 30, 2007.

U.S. Department of Defense Task Force on Mental Health. *An Achievable Vision: Report of the Department of Defense Task Force on Mental Health.* Falls Church, VA: Defense Health Board, 2007.

U.S. Government Printing Office. "Title 10—Armed Forces." January 8, 2004. http://www.access.gpo.gov/uscode/title10/title10.html. Accessed January 15, 2006.

U.S. White House. "President Holds Prime Time News Conference." October 11, 2001. http://www.whitehouse.gov/news/releases/2001/10/20011011-7.html. Accessed March 13, 2006.

Ursano, Robert J., and Ann E. Norwood, eds. *Emotional Aftermath of the Persian Gulf War: Veterans, Families, Communities, and Nations.* Washington, DC: American Psychiatric Press, 1996.

"The War in Iraq and World War II Have Now Both Lasted Three Years, Eight Months and Seven Days." *Washington Post,* November 26, 2006, B04.

Washington Post. "Faces of the Fallen." http://projects.washingtonpost.com/fallen/page1/. Accessed July 30, 2007.

Walzer, Michael. *Spheres of Justice.* New York: Basic Books, 1983.

Wickham, John A. Interview by Michael Musheno and Susan Ross. May 5, 2006.

Wong, Leonard, Thomas A. Kolditz, Raymond A. Millen, and Terrance M. Potter. *Why They Fight: Combat Motivation in the Iraq War.* Carlisle Barracks, PA: U.S. Army War College, 2003.

Wood, Sara. "Defense Department Releases Finding of Mental Health Assessment." *American Forces Press Service,* May 4, 2007. http://www.defenselink.mil/news/newsarticle.aspx?id=33055. Accessed May 5, 2007.

Wooten, Evan M. "Banging on the Backdraft Door: The Constitutional Validity of Stop-Loss in the Military." *William and Mary Law Review* 47 (2005): 1063–1109.

Yanow, Dvora. "Neither Rigorous or Objective? Interrogating Criteria for Knowledge Claims in Interpretive Science." In *Interpretation and Method: Empirical Research Methods and the Interpretive Turn,* edited by Dvora Yanow and Peregrine Schwartz-Shea, 67–88. London: Sharpe, 2006.

Young, Iris Marion. *Justice and the Politics of Difference.* Princeton: Princeton University Press, 1990.

Zinsmeister, Karl. *Boots on the Ground: A Month with the 82nd Airborne in the Battle for Iraq.* New York: Truman Talley, 2003.

Zurcher, Louis A., Jr. "The Naval Reservist: An Empirical Assessment of Ephemeral Role Enactment." *Social Forces* 53 (1977): 753–68.

Filmography

Best Years of Our Lives. DVD. Directed by William Wyler. MGM, 1946.

Born on the Fourth of July. DVD. Directed by Oliver Stone. Universal Studios, 1989.

Courage Under Fire. DVD. Directed by Edward Zwick. Twentieth Century Fox, 1996.

Death before Dishonor. DVD. Directed by Terry Leonard. Anchor Bay, 1987.

Fahrenheit 9/11. DVD. Directed by Michael Moore. Lions Gate Films, 2004.

Forrest Gump. DVD. Directed by Robert Zemeckis. Paramount Pictures, 1994.

Jarhead. DVD. Directed by Sam Mendes. Universal Studios, 2005.

The Man in the Grey Flannel Suit. DVD. Directed by Nunnally Johnson. Twentieth Century Fox, 1956.

M*A*S*H. DVD. Directed by Alan Alda, Hy Averback, Jackie Cooper, Charles S. Dubin, Burt Metcalfe, and Gene Reynolds. Twentieth Century Fox, 1972–83.

Rambo: First Blood, Part II. Directed by George Cosmatos. Live/Artisan, 1985.

The War Tapes. DVD. Directed by Deborah Scranton. Senart Films/Scranton-Lacy Films, 2006.

We Were Soldiers. DVD. Directed by Randall Wallace. Icon Entertainment, 2002.

When I Came Home. DVD. Directed by Dan Lohaus. Lohaus Films, 2006.

Why We Fight. DVD. Directed by Eugene Jarecki. Sony, 2006.

Index